Praise for *Losing Culture*

Losing Culture is about nostalgia, combining self-reflection and rich ethnographic examples from Africa and Asia with a critical view of the disciplinary anxieties of anthropology. Nostalgia, in this wonderful book, is treated as one more thing that is, in our tormented world, no longer what it used to be.

—Arjun Appadurai,
author of *The Future as Cultural Fact:
Essays on the Global Condition*

David Berliner stands at the crossroads, observing the natives, the philosophers, the heritage bureaucrats, the tourists, and other anthropologists as well, from all nationalities, when they come to look at—or even live—the past in the present. But what does he become himself? A cultural chameleon? When you have read *Losing Culture*, perhaps your anthropology will never be the same again.

—Ulf Hannerz,
author of *Writing Future Worlds:
An Anthropologist Explores Global Scenarios*

By linking the chameleon figure of the anthropologist with the theme of nostalgia, Berliner demonstrates anthropologists' important role in disabusing the general public of the illusion that "cultures" can be rebuilt in their original form. This subtle departure from conventional studies of heritage places a new and desirable emphasis on the ethical choices facing anthropologists when confronted with the politics of contested pasts. Of particular value is the unusual but well-grounded comparative perspective that Berliner draws from his findings in West Africa and Southeast Asia.

—Michael Herzfeld,
author of *Siege of the Spirits:
Community and Polity in Bangkok*

Losing Culture

The morning ceremony of almsgiving to the monks (Tak Baad), Luang Prabang, Lao PDR.

Losing Culture

~

Nostalgia, Heritage, and Our Accelerated Times

DAVID BERLINER

TRANSLATED BY DOMINIC HORSFALL

Rutgers University Press

New Brunswick, Camden, and Newark, New Jersey, and London

Library of Congress Cataloging-in-Publication Data
Names: Berliner, David, author.
Title: Losing culture : nostalgia, heritage, and the anthropologist
in accelerated times / David Berliner ; translated by Dominic Horsfall.
Other titles: Perdre sa culture. English
Description: New Brunswick, New Jersey : Rutgers University Press, [2020] |
Translation of: Perdre sa culture. | Includes bibliographical
references. | Summary: "Many people talk about how we're "losing
everything"—our culture, our traditions, our roots. As calls for
cultural preservation multiply across the globe, anthropology teaches us
that there are different ways of thinking about loss, memory,
transmissions, and heritage. In this short book, translated from the
French for the first time, David Berliner contemplates what the role of
the anthropologist should be in a world obsessed with maintaining the
past, while also rocketing toward the future"—Provided by publisher.
Identifiers: LCCN 2019034579 | ISBN 9781978815353 (paperback) |
ISBN 9781978815377 (epub)
Subjects: LCSH: Cultural property—Protection. | Collective memory. |
Group identity. | Cultural diplomacy. | Anthropology.
Classification: LCC CC135 .B4713 2020 | DDC 363.6/9—dc23
LC record available at https://lccn.loc.gov/2019034579

A British Cataloging-in-Publication record for
this book is available from the British Library.

Originally published as *Perdre sa culture* in 2018 by Editions Zones sensibles

⊚ The paper used in this publication meets the requirements of the
American National Standard for Information Sciences—Permanence of
Paper for Printed Library Materials, ANSI Z39.48-1992.

www.rutgersuniversitypress.org

Manufactured in the United States of America

In the memory of my grandmother, Rosa Hamel

It is a strange grief... To die of nostalgia for
something you will never live.
—Alessandro Barrico

Why should I care about future generations—
what have they ever done for me?
—Groucho Marx

Tu t'souviens de jours anciens et tu pleures.
(You remember old days and cry.)
—Serge Gainsbourg

Contents

Losing Culture

Introduction

The Loss of Culture and the Desire to Transmit It Onward

Where are the snows of yesteryear?...Where are our heroes
of yesteryear?...Where are our learned scholars of yesteryear?
What will become of our pedagogy of yesteryear?...Where is
our habitat of yesteryear?...Where are the politicians and
stars of yesteryear?...Where are the lords of yesteryear?
—Michel Serres, *Times of Crisis*

Let us begin with four vignettes.

2015: Alain Finkielkraut's latest pamphlet, *L'identité malheu-reuse*, soars to the top of the sales charts in bookshops across the French-speaking world. Loaded with cultural nostalgia for French exceptionalism and warmth, it trumpets a fear of contemporary change, toward immigration and Islam in particular, and denounces globalization for leading us inexorably down the path of uniformity and oblivion. With its contempt for sociologists and its problematic revisionism of Lévi-Strauss, the text is an example of French declinism, and its commercial success is far from trivial.

December 2008: Luang Prabang, a UNESCO World Heritage Site in northern Laos. Three Dutch tourists talk among themselves inside the walls of the Vat Nong temple, one of thirty-four monasteries in this holy Buddhist town. As they leave the temple, one declares forlornly, "It's a shame. Locals don't even wear their traditional clothes anymore."

2001: I find myself in the maritime region of Basse-Côte in Guinea-Conakry, Africa. In response to my questions about his parents' religious past, during the pre-Islamic time of custom, a young man in his twenties tells me, "There is nothing left here. Nothing has been passed down to us. We, the young, don't know anything about the custom."

March 2008: Finally back in Paris, at the UNESCO headquarters. An American anthropologist turned official of the Center for the Safeguarding of Intangible Cultural Heritage declares, "What we're doing here is transmitting what cannot be transmitted anymore or not well!"

But what do Finkielkraut's treatise, the discourse of these tourists, the young Guineans, and this UNESCO official all have in common? Despite stemming from different social and cultural environments, do they not all proclaim together that cultures are being lost and that cultural transmission no longer works as it should? Indeed, diagnoses of cultural loss are growing around the world. The purpose of this book is to refine our understanding of how cultural loss manifests today in different contexts, and in particular to examine the rhetorical forms that lead to this diagnosis. The concepts used here are especially important for social scientists, heritage scholars, experts in memory and museum studies, historians, and psychoanalysts, but anyone interested in how we position ourselves to meet the future with regard to the past will find the book useful.

Losing-Everything

We might call it a contemporary "losing-everything." "We're losing our culture"; "We're abandoning our customs"; "Traditions are being lost"; "Everything's being swept away"; "There's nothing left of the past"; "The young have no more interest in knowing elders' stories"; loss today comes in many forms. The loss of culture, identity, tradition, knowledge, and roots, and the consequences thereof, constitute a theme nostalgically invoked by many individuals and groups. Nostalgia, this "reaction against the irreversible," as Vladimir Jankélévitch eloquently puts it,[1] represents a fascinating angle from which to study contemporary questions of identity and culture in these times of "accelerism."[2] At first glance, nostalgia constitutes a painful feeling born of the idea that human temporality is irreversible, and that a return to the past is impossible.[3] There do exist, however, various nostalgic tonalities that bring into play a number of cognitive and emotional investments. Certain forms of nostalgia are more or less removed from intense feelings, such as the bittersweet memories I have of unique moments in my childhood, though I have no particular desire to revive them. Some feel nostalgia for places and times unconnected to their roots, like French philosopher Barbara Cassin, raised in Paris, and of Hungarian-Jewish descent, yet who feels an uncontrollable nostalgia for Corsica.[4] Nostalgia can also be completely disassociated from personal experiences. Here I think of my yearning for May 1968, an idealized intellectual age (associated with smoke-filled lecture halls and sexual freedom) that I never actually personally lived through. Across the world, young patriots are nostalgic for a country they have never known, and which probably never existed. And I am always surprised at my students' enthusiasm for types of music—such as punk or '70s rock—that belong more to my parents' generation. There is also nostalgia in the absence of nostalgic feelings, a technique abundantly used in business and commercial advertisements to sell past forms and images to be consumed.[5]

On this basis, Michael Herzfeld wisely invented the concept of "structural nostalgia" to describe this "melancholy longing"[6] for an idealized past characterized by its "replicability in every succeeding generation,"[7] and which serves today's political and moral alibis. In turn, Renato Rosaldo defines "imperialist nostalgia" as the "mourning for what One Has Destroyed,"[8] by which he refers to the primitivist nostalgia of the first anthropologists who lamented the disappearance of societies under the yoke of their colonizers, a point of view I will explore later on. Finally, Arjun Appadurai describes the propensity of individuals to mourn something they themselves did not lose as "armchair nostalgia."[9] A very useful heuristic notion, armchair nostalgia can be seen in heritage and tourism, particularly as an anxiety, now shared by heritage experts and many tourists, of losing cultural diversity, "that nostalgia for the country which we do not know" evoked by Baudelaire in *Invitation to the Voyage*[10] and the vestiges of the past when faced with the ruptures of history.

As we shall see in the second chapter, nostalgia represents a *force majeure* of heritage. The irreversibility of time, and lamentations on what one, or others, have lost, do indeed seem to be two fundamental sides of the contemporary notion of loss in the West. The 1960s and '70s, two decades of great social upheaval in Europe and the United States, saw a veritable culture of nostalgia taking shape.[11] A nostalgic frenzy glorifying the lifestyles and objects of the past can be seen today in the growing popularity of vintage clothes, flea markets, historical TV shows, organic food, retro cellphones and cameras, supposed "natural" birthing techniques, eco-museums, rustic tourism, and so on; this retromania is even encroaching on new technology (for example, how Instagram makes photos appear instantly nostalgic[12]). And, not to be outdone, the entertainment industry is inundated with hark-back productions as well, from *Mad Men* to *Downton Abbey*, by way of the new *Star Wars* episodes. "We live in a pop age gone loco for retro and crazy for commemoration," writes Simon Reynolds.[13] In our nostalgia-consuming society[14] reigns the creed of "It was better before," a perspective that Michel Serres discredits with great humor.[15]

Cultural Loss as a Political Weapon

It is this current climate of losing-everything that has brought the notions of culture, heritage, and authenticity—that great obsession of the Moderns—together into an indissoluble triumvirate, turning them into moral justifications in and of themselves, surrounded by an aura of evidence and authority. Faced with the destructive power of runaway globalization, transmission to future generations, so precious because it is under threat, has now become a *value*, both personal and political. Similarly, the imperative to find one's "roots"—the notion of the powerful arboreal metaphor that Maurizio Bettini underlines[16]—has become a moral and political injunction, in that "we must know where we came from in order to move forward," as the popular dictate tells us. Failing which, one is rootless, abnormal. "Do we know how, and are we even able to, transmit anymore?" worries the French philosopher Alain Finkielkraut,[17] whose ubiquitous interventions in the media peddle a nostalgia for a bygone France combined with his demands for the cultural integration of migrants.[18] The same "reactionary nostalgia" is found in journalist Eric Zemmour's public ranting against multicultural policies and the so-called ethnicization of France.[19]

The invocation of culture and its necessary transmission in contemporary politics is indeed widespread. Politicians call upon the trope of "losing culture" to express all sorts of hate and discrimination, as when Donald Trump claims that Europe is "losing its culture" because of immigration.[20] In the United States, the white supremacists, with their swastikas and Confederate flags, are under the impression that "white culture" is threatened by other ethnic groups. The same discourse is found in Europe, with regional variants and different intensities, where many emphasize their fear of losing their local culture, threatened by the presence of other cultural minorities (Muslims in particular). One need only think of the heated debates surrounding Europe's Christian roots,[21] and the turbulent discussions on secularism (*laïcité*), a French legacy that, from an American perspective, can often mask nationalist and Islamophobic agendas.[22] It is not for me to pathologize the human need to transmit one's own culture down to the next generation, but it is hard to ignore the growing importance afforded it among certain political elites. Who are those designated "cultural losers" (and by whom?)? Suburban youths from immigrant families? Migrants and exiles? The rural poor? Ethnic minorities? Or even, farther afield, Africans? Papuans? Who are the "cultureless" and "rootless" of today? On closer inspection, transmission of culture and discourses about it are an exercise of power, as Walter Benjamin aptly put it: "There has never been a document of culture, which is not simultaneously one of barbarism. And just as it is itself not free from barbarism, neither is it free from the process of transmission, in which it falls from one set of hands into another."[23]

Recognizing Cultural Loss

While anthropologists are increasingly uneasy with these patrimonialist ideas, they are also invoked by many individuals and groups as part of what Axel Honneth calls "struggles for recognition."[24] Most of the time, the intention behind the desire to transmit culture forward is self-affirmation in a context of globalization and social discrimination. Consider the success of Alex Haley's *Roots* in the United States, heritage tourism,[25] and the contemporary fad for genealogy and DNA research; but also the demands of Australian and American indigenous populations as well as immigrant families in Europe for the preservation of their cultures; while the citizens of Quebec made their famous "Je me souviens" (I remember) their regional motto. In fact, culture and heritage may be considered as "a resource and a weapon for affirming identity, dignity, power before nation states or the international community."[26] Often, those who demand the right to have their culture recognized as transmissible heritage are themselves historical victims,[27] for example, the descendants of those who have known the torments of the "Black condition,"[28] or children of genocide victims.[29] In a powerful text, French anthropologist Nicole Lapierre shows how the Jews of Plock survived the Holocaust between impossible words and intolerable forgetting, and it is precisely this "painful, haunted in-between" that "alone can be transmitted,"[30] a feeling described by Georges Perec when, on a visit to Ellis Island in 1979, he experiences this lack of transmission since he does not speak his parents' language or share any of their memories.[31] The survivors and descendants of populations that have been colonized, discriminated against, and exterminated, be they aboriginal Australians, or the colonized peoples of Congo or the Americas,[32] seek to transmit the memories of their experiences and their traumatic heritage.[33] For many also, the too-oft-criticized "duty to remember" represents a legitimate demand on behalf of millions of individuals to see their trauma recognized and commemorated. Yet, while silence has often gone hand in hand with trauma, the experience of loss, whether real or vicarious, is complemented by an imperative to transmit a culture made valuable by the fact of having been the object of destruction. Transmission, for many of these historical victims, is the preservation of the memory of this trauma into modernity, but also the preservation of their culture. How to separate these two dimensions that destruction has made inseparable?

Loss, a Zeitgeist

And yet the desire to transmit goes far beyond these groups of victims. Nowadays it also includes cultural discourses and practices that serve as a vehicle for a lament on the disappearance-in-progress, and the means to counter it, and bear witness above all to fear. Fear of change? Of the acceleration of time? Of individualism? Of hybridization? Or even that globalization will lead to eradication? But what is it we are afraid of losing? In truth, I am not sure that we always know what we would prefer not to lose. In the West, this "losing-everything" rhetoric, where "the past has become a project . . . nostalgia a program,"[34] is all too apparent in today's prevailing crisis-based discourse. The tone is pre-apocalyptic. In contemporary catastrophism, contrarily to Michelet's famous epigraph "Each epoch dreams of the one to follow,"[35] the present has *always already* been invaded by a terrible future. The worst yet to come is no longer fantasy but rather "a category of experience."[36]

It should be noted that contemporary thought makes abundant use of end-of-the-world rhetoric: *The End of History* (Fukuyama 1992), *The End of the Village* (Le Goff 2012), or indeed *The End of*

Societies (Touraine 2013). Bruno Latour also adopts a pre-apocalyptic tone intended to alert the world to the risk of the destruction of the environment (2013), having recently declared that "the apocalypse is our opportunity."[37] "We are no longer the inheritors," the French anthropologist David Le Breton writes anxiously. "Social, intergenerational, or cultural divisions are making the world more confused, more uncertain."[38] What state will we leave the world in to our children and grandchildren, already thought of as passive and disillusioned? What, moreover, would humanity be without UNESCO's efforts to transmit our heritage to future generations? Would we not have a world subject to chaos and widespread discord, like at the dawn of an impending cataclysm? And so it is out of fear of disappearance, for the children of the future, that we seek to preserve, to "museumify" ways of life, values, traditions, traumatic memories, identities, roots, languages, rites, skills, and so on, and also the earth as an ecosystem. In this "age of nostalgia," as Zygmunt Bauman calls it in his last book *Retrotopia*, when faced with losing everything, something of the past must absolutely be carried forward, of identities and cultures, whether our own or those of others.[39] Between denouncing the dramatic effects of unfettered capitalism and the fantasy of the apocalypse there is a very thin line that is not always easy to see.

Exonostalgias

Despite being more apparent now due to greater awareness of environmental risk,[40] this "heritage crusade"[41] is nothing new. The history of heritage is the history of conservation for future generations. In the first book of his *Histories*, Herodotus of Halicarnassus was already concerned with "preserving from decay the remembrance of what men have done, and of preventing the great and wonderful actions of the Greeks and the Barbarians from losing their due meed of glory."[42] During the nineteenth century, conservation policies accompanied the nationalist strategies of the European states, where an elite sense of loss prevailed in the midst of runaway industrialization and urbanization, fueling a desire to patrimonialize and museumify,[43] and stimulating scientific and literary interest in memory and loss.[44] For Western anthropologists, the period before the Second World War was a golden age of modernist nostalgia for other worlds, near or far, on the verge of being lost forever under threat from modernization.[45] In 1961 still, Claude Lévi-Strauss suggested that anthropology would be called "entropology," a "discipline that devotes itself to the study of this process of disintegration in its most highly evolved forms."[46] In the second and third chapters of this book, I explore this very particular point of view, which I call *exonostalgia*.

Exonostalgia constitutes nostalgia for a past not experienced personally. Unlike episodic memory, which connects individuals viscerally to their past,[47] allowing them to return in their minds to events that they have lived, this vicarious nostalgia encompasses a variety of affects and discourses related to loss, but detached from direct experience. Like the notion of "prosthetic" memory developed by Alison Landsberg,[48] such regret is often projected through films or museums, and in schools. While there are different types of exonostalgias, the one I propose to explore in this book is the sadness for *other people's* cultural loss. Take for instance the French TV show *Rendez-vous en terre inconnue* (in which journalist Frédéric Lopez takes celebrities to meet traditional societies) and the works of Jared Diamond (his book *The World until Yesterday*, in particular). They perpetuate the classic tropes of the endangered good savage, and of cultural heritage in decline; a modernist search (already described by Montaigne in the sixteenth century) for faraway, authentic tribes, these paradise cultures under threat of extinction, where sincerity, respect for nature, purity, solidarity, innocence, and emotion were thought to prevail. An expedition to the heart of old Western stereotypes steeped in a "nostalgia for the primitive," it is the very same that once fueled colonial paternalism and anthropology, and lingers on in the way we talk about others, especially distant others.

Nowadays, such exonostalgic fervor exists on a global scale, notably in the existence of international organizations like UNESCO.[49] Although they are more fragmented than we might expect, UNESCO's actions are contributing to the worldwide dissemination of the trope of disappearing culture. Far from being innocuous, these globalized discourses about cultural loss produce real effects, from appropriate heritage policies to feeding cultural essentialism and nationalism. They are sometimes perceived as patronizing, and contested by members of communities who do not feel they are losing their culture.[50] They often lead to conflicts of interpretation surrounding what is and is not legitimate heritage, as I will demonstrate in the second chapter of this book.

However, in the midst of such a declinist zeitgeist, anthropologists have some new perspectives to offer. First of all, they study, from the inside, how human societies problematize, in myriad different ways, the question of cultural loss and how individuals express themselves about it. Second, they aim at developing theoretical models to grasp cultural transmission and to confirm the diagnosis of loss.

What People Claim to Have Lost

Each individual needs a cultural legacy to pass on, without which, as the American anthropologist Edward Sapir once wrote, he "is reduced to impotence. He is incapable, on his own, depending on his intellectual resources and personal strength alone, to build a resistant, living cultural framework."[51] What remains to be seen is what exactly this indispensable cultural legacy is made of. This is not to deny what is evident: cultural transmission is indeed a core human (and animal[52]) trait. It binds individuals together and makes the perpetuation of culture possible. Humans create stories and practices that serve to stabilize both their own individual identities and that of their group. However, it would be dogmatic to think that these same stories are necessarily those that round out the narratives of national and territorial roots, and that these practices belong only to those national cultures deemed legitimate. It is also problematic to think that there is only one way of transmitting culture. Here, things are much more complicated. First of all, not all human societies have considered the question of loss and transmission in the same way. Thinking about memory and disappearance comes in different forms. When a UNESCO expert, a Guatemalan peasant, an American activist, and an academic from Burkina Faso all claim to have lost their culture, their assertions should all be considered in the context of their local—albeit now globally interconnected—representations and practices.

As I demonstrate in the first chapter, the discourse among the Bulongic people of Guinea-Conakry on the loss of their customs is based on a social configuration linked to secrecy. Loss there is the loss of power of the old men, who, in turn, refuse to transmit their knowledge to younger generations. This is a discourse that clashes with the often pessimistic, patrimonialist rhetoric of the urban elites beginning to spread through the villages of this region. Indeed, it is often specific categories of actors who diagnose loss in the first place. My second case study, based on my ongoing research in northern Laos since 2007, describes how an international community of loss comes to be built. In Luang Prabang, Laos, a variety of discourses thrives on cultural transmission and its associated crisis—a situation that reveals the conflicts of interpretation between the nostalgic discourses and practices of UNESCO experts and those of the local actors, who, for the most part, do not feel any sense of loss (and are often depicted by the former as cultural incompetents). This book explores in earnest the motives of the actors and groups involved vis-à-vis cultural loss and the processes of transmission. Representations of loss and transmission are spread and consolidated in every group: notions about what is lost, what should be transmitted, how this should be done, and to what end. I intend to set out a thorough exposition of local theories, and take into account the reflexive discourses of the actors on the conditions of loss and persistence.

Anthropology and Cultural Transmission

To question loss and its various diagnoses is, of course, to question cultural transmission and its mechanisms. In its broadest sense, cultural transmission, those processes which, by binding individuals together, serve to perpetuate a group, is a problem as old as anthropology itself, found in even the earliest texts of our discipline.[53] One need only think of the "survivals" of Edward Burnett Tylor, who, though admittedly shrouded in a thick evolutionist fog, sought to understand the persistence of the past in the present, the challenge of ethnography to expose, in his view, "the remains of crude old culture which have passed into harmful superstition."[54] A few decades later, this idea of the past "passing" into the present can readily be found in most classical definitions of culture (especially in the American school), almost always linked to questions of how it is transmitted and learned.[55] With regard to this idea, the concept of "culture" is not isolated. The same goes for the notion of "tradition," another key idea that occupies a choice position in the conceptual panoply of generations of anthropologists. Yes, tradition too is transmitted and lost. In his unbeatable article, "Techniques of the Body," Marcel Mauss highlights the natural link between tradition and transmission ("Once formed, tradition is what is transmitted") and states: "There is no technique and no transmission in the absence of tradition. This above all is what distinguishes man from the animals: the transmission of his techniques and very probably their oral transmission,"[56] an idea now contested by ethologists and primatologists. More recently, Jean Pouillon defines tradition as "what from the past persists into the present, where it is transmitted and remains active and is accepted by those who have received it and who, in turn, over the generations, pass it on."[57] And even when certain traditions can be re-created and fictitious, they still involve the transmission of elements of the past into the present. As Eric J. Hobsbawm notes, invented tradition "automatically implies continuity with the past. In fact, where possible, [such traditions] normally attempt to establish continuity with a suitable historic past."[58] Everything always comes back to transmission . . .

When reading the founding texts of anthropology, we would do well to note one of the fundamental questions raised therein: that of continuity, of the perpetuation of the cultural, of its transmission, and of loss. To consider the state of a cultural configuration or social order and, by extension, the persistence across time of this order (or of certain dimensions of this order), from the past to the present; "to stabilize the social," to borrow Bruno Latour's phrase,[59] and invoke its transformative durability, its metamorphic solidity, and, I would suggest, its transmissibility (or that of some of its traits) is at the very heart of our approach. "How are social forms maintained?" asked Georg Simmel back in 1898. There are some who see in anthropology (and rightly so) a "science of continuity"[60] that focuses on *what lasts* and rests on stable formations, a point of view supported in 1952 by Radcliffe-Brown, for whom "one of the fundamental theoretical problems . . . is that of the nature of social continuity."[61] We need only consider Pierre Bourdieu,[62] Fredrik Barth,[63] Marshall Sahlins,[64] Jack Goody,[65] and Philippe Descola,[66] whose respective theories—habitus, generative approach to cultural transmission, mythopraxis, creative reconstruction, schemas of practice—feature among the most key ideas in contemporary anthropology. Do they not repeatedly embody this anthropological imperative to theorize cultural persistence while taking into account social transformations? How then should we not see transmission of culture as the "left-unsaid" in these texts, all of which lead us to contemplate the "presence of the past in the present?" As French anthropologist Isac Chiva put it quite succinctly, "Ethnologists are concerned with two things: how groups differ between one another and how they ensure their own continuity while maintaining these differences."[67]

Assessing Loss, Describing Transmission

However, research about the very *processes* involved in cultural transmission and loss is scarce. There is still much ground to clear to better understand why practices and representations continue to be, or are lost.[68] How then do we tackle the elusive realities that are cultural loss and cultural transmission? Where does transmitting begin? Do we describe it as an ongoing process, or should we only convey its effects, a posteriori? How to grasp and quantify cultural loss? First of all, studying cultural transmission and loss is a *theoretical posture*. Describing the cultural phenomena of loss and transmission requires us above all to recognize that some concepts, practices, and emotions of the past are not automatically carried forward into the present, and to identify the lengthy processes by which they pass between generations and are appropriated by those who acquire them. To demonstrate this passing-on and its absence is to set a very complex scene; to pinpoint its *mediators*: actors, institutions, actions, interactions, places, ideologies, critical moments, smells, texts, silences, ordinary moments, sounds, emotions, objects, and technologies. Anthropologists bent on transmission and loss must seek out the mediums, contexts, categories of actor, mental processes, interactions, and materialities by which transference is made possible or not. They situate themselves on the level where these practices are performed, within the very fabric of social interactions, acts of communication, and cognitive processes; and they seek to demonstrate how ways of acting, feeling, or thinking are transmitted and learned. Who transmits what, and how? What networks of transmission, forms of organization, and ideologies is this kind of heritage built upon?

While people hold their own experiences and theories of transmission and loss, anthropologists set up models of what they think "actually" happens, sometimes highlighting the discrepancy that can exist between people's interpretations and scholarly models.[69] Often, the scene for cultural transmission and loss works behind people's considerations. In most instances, individuals are being acted on by implicit transmission processes, which they creatively engage with, usually without thinking about them explicitly. As Bourdieu captured in Kabyle society, not all transmission is informed by expressed and explicit prescriptions. Rather, every society is constituted through processes of transmission "that go without saying." These linguistic interjections or silences, these emotional expressions, these seemingly insignificant gestures, tones, and actions in daily interactions all act on individuals, and contribute, often implicitly, to instilling "a whole cosmology, an ethic, a metaphysic, a political philosophy."[70] In short, transmission of culture, through language, actions, gestures, and emotions, "occurs without thinking" and most of the time "impels people without their knowledge."[71]

Above all, these phenomena are diverse and creative. The instances of failure, stalling, reinterpretation, and re-creation are myriad. They never occur the same way twice. They fall within the dynamic shifts of history. On this subject, we should take into account their entanglement with temporality.[72] As a matter of fact, diagnoses of and remedies against loss take place within very specific ontological temporalities, which give cultural transmission its style, possibilities, and constraints. Suffice it to think of post-Holocaust diasporic Jews (whose temporality is centered around the frightening premise of a future recurrence of their persecution) or millenarist movements, which hold their own temporalities for transmission and have particular views on the diagnosis of its crisis. Vlad Naumescu, who studies the traumatic history of Orthodox Old Believers in Romania, cut off from the Russian Orthodox Church in the seventeenth century, reminds us, for example, of the paramount importance of localizing, in historical terms, transmission of culture, its discourses and practices—in this case a collective of individuals who see, in the crisis of transmission currently affecting their community, a confirmation of their apocalyptic beliefs.[73]

The landscape of cultural transmission and loss is itself the result of complex historical processes. As anthropologists, one of our intellectual endeavors consists in resituating the chain of transmission in the midst of such historical contingencies. In this regard, it is equally crucial for us to investigate how and why people decide to stop performing cultural practices, or why and how some lost interest in them. This leads me to think in particular of the Ghanaian Pentecostals studied by Birgit Meyer, who consider their relationship with the past in terms of total rupture;[74] or the Bulongic I met in Guinea-Conakry, who believe that the abandonment of their pre-Islamic practices in the 1950s was the result of a generational choice intended to allow them to embrace Guinean modernity through the introduction of Islam.

In his *Major Trends in Jewish Mysticism*, borrowing a story from the Jewish Hasidic tradition of Eastern Europe, Gershom Sholem provides a fine example of the vagaries of transmission. Whenever the Baal Shem Tov, an eighteenth-century rabbi and founder of Hasidism, had a difficult task to accomplish, he would go to a specific location in the forest, light a fire, and pray. His successors were pious men, still endowed with extensive Judaic knowledge, but forgot the prayer and how to light a fire. As a result, subsequent generations of rabbis no longer said the Baal Shem Tov's prayer, lit a fire, or even knew where to pray, but continued nonetheless to tell this story as a way of honoring God.[75] So which is it, loss or transmission? Continuity versus rupture? This is all that transmission and loss as *questions* can bring to our reflection on contemporary societies. By being at the heart of historical processes, they call into question the way in which we describe what is real, and, beyond the rhetoric of contemporary losing-everything, provide the basis of a reflection on the continuity of human societies faced with the ruptures of history.

The Plastic Anthropologist and Cultural Loss

Finally, in the last chapter of this book, drawing on accounts of ethnographic experiences, I look at anthropologists themselves and their epistemological relationship with cultural loss. As I have said, anthropologists have historically been obsessed with the cultural loss of *others*, a form of exonostalgia that they have cherished from the foundation of our discipline. By contrast, it is interesting to note how little thought has been given to the risk of loss that they expose themselves to in their research, especially in participant observation. Thus I propose to examine the cognitive, emotional, and epistemological aspects of cultural loss on the phenomenological, individual level of the anthropological experience. A rich body of literature exists on the mimetic processes of cultural assimilation within the context of European colonialism. Inspired by Aristotle, the notion of mimesis used by Taussig[76] and Stoller[77] sheds light on how colonized peoples appropriated the colonizer's otherness, thereby challenging it. For these authors, mimesis constitutes above all a possibility of resistance for the colonized, an idea also expounded by Homi Bhabha, by which colonialism sustained the dilemma of the relationship between the original and the copy.[78] Indeed, in the colonial context, the colonizer seeks to civilize the natives while at the same time denying them access to the position of the colonizer. As Albert Memmi provocatively writes, "The better [the colonized] imitates, . . . the more the colonizer becomes irritated."[79] The latter fears the mimetic abilities of the colonized. At the same time, imitation, both parodically and ironically, allows for a form of indigenous destabilization, mocking and criticizing the colonizer by aping him. But this imitative gamble also affects the colonizer, who risks losing his own identity by not maintaining the right distance between himself and the natives. For fear of "going native," of losing oneself and one's culture, colonists were encouraged to limit social contact with the locals and even avoid imitating their forms of dress.[80] One need only think of Kurtz, the ivory dealer in Conrad's *Heart of Darkness*, who became both physically and psychologically damaged by having stayed too long in the jungle, in close contact with its inhabitants.

These questions are central to ethnographic practice. As we know, going native does represent an epistemological, ethical, and existential issue for most anthropologists—a line not to be crossed, we might say. Prone to nostalgia, anthropologists are also, by definition, those who tack back and forth from one cultural horizon to another. And yet they do not lose their culture. On the contrary, they are fueled by multiple influences and identifications. Sometimes, researchers do lose themselves in the field, but, in the accounts I will review, they return to themselves, "from anguish to exultation."[81] In the course of their research, anthropologists deliberately engage their mimetic as well as empathic and play-based competences. In the very act of participant observation they expose themselves to temporary situations of disidentity. In qualifying them as "plastic,"[82] I mean that they learn to master these mechanisms of leaving and returning to the self, these arts of passing (to use Harold Garfinkel's notion), whereby loss is always a risk if one is to make the most of the ethnographic field, this process of acquiring new knowledge and skills. It is this strange aspect of our discipline that I intend to map out in the final chapter of this book, drawing inspiration not from the classics of postcolonial literature, but from philosophical and psychological studies on imitation and acting—a strange method indeed to reveal oneself a human chameleon, an expert in the reversible permutation of one's identity, whose mimetic abilities lead not to loss, but attest above all to one's plasticity.

1
Transmission Impossible in West Africa

> But what would Africa be without fetishes and their mysteries?
> —Achille Mbembe, *Critique de la raison nègre*

The Mask behind the Glass

Africa—its memory and its objects. Inside a glass display case, African objects have the power to fascinate. One day, I found myself discussing the famous snakelike Baga[1] mask (known as the *bansonyi* in Europe and the United States) with a friend, an enthusiast for non-European art. We were in a museum, standing in front of a glass case containing this particular mask. My friend described the *bansonyi* in terms of an object, a material reality, solid, inanimate, tangible, manmade, visible, and so on; but beautiful, fragile, and precious, he emphasized, pointing out the aesthetic quality of its design, as well as potential problems it might have with paintwork and cracking. It was a "rare object" in light of its pedigree and this or that distinctive feature; an "authentic object" for having been collected before 1920; an "aesthetic object," whose forms inspired Matisse and Giacometti; and a "valuable object" on the African art market since its acquisition from a famous collector; but always just an object, of pure materiality, to be displayed center stage. As the focus of my friend's gaze and passions, the *bansonyi* (objectified by use of the definite article) evoked a veritable object mystique, which only served to reinforce the museological impetus. Always referring to the *bansonyi* as an object, my friend began to utter a few generalities on the symbolic resonance of the snake in West Africa; that this mask must certainly be the illustration of a mythology; and that it "served to," "was made to," express this mythical background. Everything he said about the object was in the past tense, nostalgic in its way: "Unfortunately, there's nothing left today among the Baga. Before, they used to carve the *bansonyi* masks, but now the masks have vanished, and the Baga are Muslim. Sadly for them, they've lost their culture." To his mind, Islamization and the loss of the object must have caused shock waves in the traditional community, an unprecedented crisis of identity for the Baga. Based on the material nature and fairly specific definition of what can be called a mask, his theory implied the absence of objects as a sign of cultural loss: if there are no more of the old objects to be found among the Baga today, or no one mentions them, it must mean that the basis of what once was is now gone. In the end, he was pleased to see the successful conservation of these memory-objects in our museums, saved from a destructive past.

And so the memory of these ancient colonized peoples is preserved through their objects, forever protected behind the plexiglass of our museums. On reflection, the materiality of these objects, their relative ability to withstand the ravages of time, has become for us a reassuring synonym for memory, permanence, and transmission of culture.[2] In contrast, the absence of visible objects signifies nondurability, an inability to transmit and perpetuate culture. Without these tangible objects and their increasing global renown, how would African societies ever be able to remember their history? Is an Islamized or Christianized African society without any visible "ancestral" rituals not a ship lost at sea—or, in less poetic terms, a society without memory?

The Silence of Masks

The Bulongic constitute one of the seven Baga subgroups along-side which I conducted my research between 1998 and 2002. There is little documentary evidence available that would allow us to ana-lyze what their religion comprised before the 1950s.[3] Broadly speaking, what my interlocutors referred to using the term "cus-tom" was an organized religion that predated the establishment of Islam, based on the existence of immaterial entities in the world (spirits) and their relationships with humans, involving certain places (sacred groves, ritual houses), ritual practices (initiation), social categories (uncircumcised/initiates/women), as well as secrets and prohibitions. Among the Bulongic featured a snake mask called Mossolo Kombo that completely dominated the lives of men, from rites of passage to manhood through initiation to punishment for misdeeds, as well as the subordination of women. In the hands of the initiated elders, it instilled a veritable climate of terror.

Starting in the 1930s, certain local leaders, particularly the can-ton chiefs (*chefs de cantons*), began to surround themselves with Muslim experts (*karamoko*) and gradually converted to Islam. The first Quranic schools began to appear in the region. In 1954, the local young boys, those now referred to as *ceux de 54*, underwent their initiation. With the arrival of a Quranic expert known as Asékou Bokaré, 1954 saw the end of local ritual and carving prac-tices, along with most other pre-Islamic practices too. This kind of destruction of objects and desecration of ritual sites, this reli-gious iconoclasm around the same time that Islam took a firm hold, has known many different guises in West Africa. There are, of course, many well-known examples of accommodation between Islam and the ritual practices that came before it;[4] but among the Bulongic, all pre-Islamic rites appear to have been incompatible with the Muslim faith. The few art historians and anthropolo-gists to take an interest in Guinea's coastal populations reported how this once culturally diverse and prosperous Bulongic society became, in the wake of these rapid religious changes, silent and forgetful. In the literature, the Bulongic (and other Baga subgroups) are always described in terms of endangered societies. According to French anthropologist Denise Paulme, the only ethnologist to have conducted research in the region prior to Guinea's independence, these populations had already become heirs to a tradition they were incapable of preserving, and she as an ethnologist was bound to witness, helplessly, the end of their story: "Threatened on all sides," she wrote, "Baga society will soon disappear. It is already too late to record the essentials."[5]

Transmission Impossible

The year 1954 saw the last male Bulongic initiation. Never again, so say the elders, would an initiation take place in the shadows of the sacred groves. The initiation masks would no longer be carved, nor would the people dance; the drums were about to fall silent. The drinking of palm wine was to stop. New dates were to be introduced into the ritual calendar, and circumcision to be conducted according to Muslim rites. Nowadays the principal guardians of their Islamic faith, the old men who lived through this final ritual, celebrate the arrival of Islam, while declaring themselves "the last Bulongic," the silent keepers of knowledge and secrets that cannot be transmitted without initiation. Judging from what they say, nothing of this past before Islam, of the time of custom, will ever be revived: transmission of this information is now impossible.

These old men always met me with a discourse marked by many silences, only confirming the nostalgic musings of my interlocutors in Europe. "We've left everything behind. There's nothing left here!" they would lament, before closing themselves off behind a wall of silence. Taking this to mean "they have nothing left to say," I first interpreted this silence in accordance with my own prejudices: they say nothing about it because they have nothing left to say about it. And this phrase "we are the last Bulongic," something I heard these old men say many times, the sad confirmation of my fears of a cultural void, spelled the doom of an Africanism that I had too much wanted to believe in. There was to be no possibility of re-creating the mask, no more trace of those great initiation rituals described by Denise Paulme in the 1950s. My disappointment during those first months of my fieldwork was considerable. Where was the Africa of our museums: the Africa of legend, from the novels of Joseph Conrad, the Africa of our grandparents, so ingrained in the imaginations of the Western colonial world?

Indeed, the younger villagers confirmed that they knew nothing of the pre-Islamic traditions; mourning the loss of these secrets that could have made them better prepared for the hazards of modernity, all of them blamed the old men and their silence. This was in fact the same lament that marked the discourse of the urban Bulongic now living in Conakry, those seeking to actively preserve their cultural heritage (by recording it, photographing it, or writing it down). In this way, under the combined blows of Islamization and the demystification policies of Sékou Touré, the religious edifice of the Bulongic appeared to have crumbled entirely—and abruptly—giving way to silence, and its (supposed) synonyms: forgetting and loss.

The Young Have Not Forgotten

And so the first months of my ethnographic experience were spent in silence, during which I felt a great deal of this "ethnographic nostalgia," so aptly described by Dimitrios Theodossopoulos as the anthropologist's desire to find continuities in the studied society with an idealized vision of a past cultural identity, often conveyed by the ethnographic texts themselves.[6] Yet, gradually, I began to realize that the actual sites of transmission were not those I had been so impatient to discover since the start of my fieldwork. In fact, there is a considerable gap between the discourses *on* transmission (what should be transmitted or not, how, and to what end) and the subtle realities of transmitting (its agents, objects, recipients, i.e., the mechanisms behind it), a divide often hard to identify in the Bulongic environment, shrouded as it was in secrecy.

Contrary to both the established credo depicting Africa's younger generations as rootless and the discourses of the elders, the younger Bulongic do not in fact lack memory. Having been born after 1954, they were never initiated, nor saw the Mossolo Kombo mask dance. They know nothing of the time when their fathers and grandfathers would only drink and dance. And yet this pre-Islamic religious past remains both apparent and valued, and the young do possess a religious memory. They have heard tell of initiation, of the powerful rites, secret locations, and prohibitions, out of which emerge a series of stereotypes in regard to custom. The young adults are all well aware that Mossolo Kombo is a very powerful and dangerous spirit, related to the sacred groves, secrets, and initiation, as well as the violence the latter entails. Indeed, says Abdou (aged twenty), "everyone was very scared of Mossolo Kombo. When he screamed, everyone had to run and lock themselves in their houses with the windows closed." As proof of his power, "whenever Mossolo Kombo would scream in the mangrove swamps, you could hear it, even here"; "he moved like light"; "he was as tall as a palm tree"; "he could get inside your pants and scream." These were just some of the things I heard from younger people in the village, the same extraordinary powers that were beneficial for rice growing and helped the Bulongic "protect themselves against their enemies during ethnic conflicts."

While the young may speak about initiation in the past tense, the present does prevail when discussing Mossolo Kombo. However, most of them are unaware that the mask had a material component, which was banned with the arrival of Asékou Bokaré in the 1950s. For them, Mossolo Kombo represents in particular a typically Bulongic spirit, autonomous and unpredictable, known only to "our" elders, and that still instills terror. For, to their minds, there is no dissolution of the continuity between the past and the present. As Oumar, aged eighteen, told me, "Mossolo Kombo is there, with his wife and children, he lives in the mangroves. You can see him down there praying. When the sun is hot on the plain and you're walking alone, you can see him." During my last visit in 2001, a group of young people told me how they had seen the spirit while preparing to cut wood in what they did not realize was an old sacred grove. They explained how Mossolo Kombo had appeared to tell them not to cut wood in this forbidden place. And several of them stressed how much "everyone still fears Mossolo Kombo, he still kills a lot. He can be found all across Bulongic country. Everything is there." And there are rumors that the initiated elders are still practicing in secret. If there is one thing that all the uninitiated young people hold true, it is that the elders still hold the secrets that made the groves sacred. "These secrets are still there"; "the elders can still do it"; "it still exists today"; "they're carrying on with Mossolo Kombo, but in secret": these are some of the things I heard them say to reinforce their point of view. In any case, it does not matter that the sacred groves were cut down during Asékou's time; the elders now go to Mecca for Hajj, described to me by Abdoulaye, a young male aged twenty, as a "place reserved specially for the elders, where all the secrets are revealed to them." Like the uninitiated who came before them, the young are acutely aware of their exclusion from this hidden knowledge, highlighting the very special bond that exists between their elders and these secrets. For the young villagers, the elders' secrets are the symbols of another time, safe and idyllic, a source of fascination, but also dangerous and frightening. Above all, however, as we shall see, this is an age waiting to be revived, though they acknowledge, paradoxically, that they are waiting for what is now an "impossible" transmission of knowledge. Far from forgetting, faced with a difficult present full of frustrations, the young seem to be weighed down "to the point of paralysis by a fixated memory."[7]

The Elders' Memory

Constrained by the dissimulation tactics of their elders, the memories of the young reveal what has been told to them, as well as the effort they have made to reimagine a world they have never known. I too became aware of this ambiguous sense of the "absent being present," of the existence of something dangerous and precious, something only the initiated elders possess, but which remains hidden away and buried. The latter are as closed off and impenetrable as their children are open and candid. In their company, I was first met with silence. This is an extremely sensitive domain, mired in taboo. Many of them would answer me with a smile, saying: "Custom? We can't talk about that, we swore not to say anything." My tactlessness was all too apparent; one simply couldn't ask direct questions on the subject of their secrets. Misjudged curiosity could be punished by death, as if the words themselves were dangerous, and survival lay in silence. "In the past," people say, "you could be reported by a palm kernel for mentioning Mossolo Kombo. Even a fly could report you." The question is then: "In what way does one not talk about it?"[8]

Despite the silences and innuendo that characterized them, the conversations I held with the initiated elders over the course of several months were nonetheless quite instructive. One thing they repeatedly stressed was the importance of having abandoned their pre-Islamic practices, initiations, and sacred groves. Their discourse exuded the rhetoric of both Islam and Sékou Touré (who ruled Guinea from 1958 to 1984, and launched demystification campaigns targeting rural communities and their "regressive" beliefs), full of moral pronouncements against so-called animist practices. The arrival of Islam was always recounted with an apologetic tone. Always keen to project an image of being respectable Muslims, their accounts described the perseverance, the passion, the courage, and the temerity of the first converts. In 1954, people had grown "tired of custom" because "fetishes stopped them moving forward. Custom was hampering progress." From the point of view of these elders, who were twenty at the time, it would seem that ritual practices had become incompatible with the demands of the present in the 1950s, at the dawn of Guinea's independence. At first, they spoke of custom in the past tense, whereas Islam was referred to in the present.

There is, however, something ambivalent in how the older Bulongic relate to custom—a sort of cognitive and moral dissonance, typical of the kind of violent and cathartic collapse of religious systems.[9] These old men simultaneously highlighted the importance of the changes that took place up to 1954; nostalgically described the era of initiation and pre-Islamic rituals as some sort of golden age and idyllic past; and lamented the real loss of ritual power that accompanied the end of this period. In fact, the abandonment of initiation is also considered by many as a weakening of the ritual vitality of Bulongic country. And they continually refer to this past, when the older Bulongic were "true" Bulongic, the bearers of secrets endowing their holders with cunning and extraordinary ritual power: "During custom, there were real men"; "the sacred grove was strong"; "back then, thanks to the sacred grove, we were the smartest people in the world." To acquire this dangerous knowledge, one had to have undergone the violence of initiation, as demonstrated by the scars that these old men showed off to me proudly during our interviews.

This is the same ambivalence, between nostalgia for the time of custom and the necessity of having abolished it, that arises with regard to Mossolo Kombo, the entity of initiation that played such a crucial role in the ritual landscape before 1954. Whenever I showed them photographs of the *bansonyi* object, the initiated elders would react stereotypically. First, they were astonished that I should have acquired such an image, and strictly refused to talk about these things, especially in front of women and children. Then, they would exclaim "Mossolo," smile, and begin to sing and speak nostalgically. All of them proved particularly discreet on this topic. Either before or after 1954, Mossolo Kombo was never spoken of in relation to the object, under pain of death. Today, as then, it remains hard to say before an uninitiated audience that the circumcising mask was, in part, a wooden artifact. The elders did, however, admit to me privately that this is what it was: "That's just a piece of wood in the photo, we carved it ourselves." Those willing to talk to me acknowledged that, since 1954, there had been no more sculptors to carve it, nor any large collective initiations or public dances at which to stage its appearance.

While discreetly acknowledging the mask's material component, the initiated elders all agree among themselves that "there is something besides the wood." Mossolo Kombo may secretly have been a carved piece of wood that was destroyed by men, but above all it was the spirit that the wood embodied. The discourse of the old men always presents Mossolo Kombo as a spirit found in the sea and in the mangrove swamps. And the spirit itself, a water spirit, has not disappeared: "Masks disappear, but the spirits remain. Mossolo Kombo still exists. You can see him if you're clever enough. He hasn't disappeared. The wood is gone, but a spirit doesn't die. There are still those that turn to him secretly." The initiated elders remain laconic on this subject yet say just enough to evoke Mossolo Kombo's presence in the form of a religious force that they alone can grasp, thanks to the time they spent in the sacred grove at the time of custom. As one old man pointed out: "Mossolo is there, the secrets are there. The people are there. When the children say that Mossolo Kombo is there, they are right. I will tell you he is there too. Mossolo Kombo is the people and a spirit. We can make him tomorrow morning. He is there because we are there. But when we're gone . . ."

Pressured by the young who invoke the loss of knowledge, the elders claim that transmission of this information is no longer possible, emphasizing the social and ritual constraints preventing transmission today. Without initiation, they say, there is no more context in which to pass down this knowledge-suffering. Because it was acquired within a highly specific context, during the lost time of custom, this knowledge is now nontransmissible. In their refusal to transmit, the initiated elders invoke, fatalistically, the degeneration of the younger Bulongic: "The young have been badly raised and don't know how to keep the secrets. They'll use them badly. Who today would even be capable of taking them on? In our day, we were well instructed in the sacred grove."

Exchanges between the young adults, convinced that there is something to be known, and the initiated elders are always characterized by distance. An atmosphere of imperviousness and suspicion reigns over intergenerational interactions nowadays. And yet these are also marked by a strange congruence. I conducted countless interviews with young people that were suddenly interrupted by an elder who had come to monopolize the conversation and force the young into silence, saying: "They don't know anything, they're children. We're the sacred grove!" Whereupon the young would defer: "It's true, we don't know anything. We never went through the grove. If anyone knows, it's him!" Not only do they acknowledge their exclusion and ignorance of this hidden knowledge; the young villagers are also the first to admit their hand in this impossible transmission. Shamefaced, they unprotestingly confess themselves "incapable," "boastful," "selfish," "disrespectful," "ill-mannered," and "ignorant"; in short, all the flaws that make them incapable of receiving in the first place.

Loss as a Loss of Power

In practice, explicit references to custom and its secrets are very seldom made among the initiates and their sons. According to my interlocutors, they do occur very occasionally in private between fathers and sons, though I never had a chance to witness these most rare and secretive interactions. However, as I remarked on several occasions, in certain public contexts there did arise some veiled references to custom and secrets. In these situations, for the initiated elders to mention initiation, Mossolo Kombo, and the power of the ancients is no mere rhetorical device for the sake of nostalgia; in fact, most of the time these veiled references serve a particular purpose, namely, to disparage the young adults' behavior and intimidate them by hinting at experiences related to the secrets that they have not lived and are forever excluded from. I remember one day, for example, a furious old man yelling at his young boys: "Don't mock me! You don't know me! I am Mossolo Kombo!" On a similar occasion, another old man, pointing at his son, exclaimed, "The young know nothing! Once upon a time, we were well taught in the grove. But they know nothing. We are the last Bulongic."

This phrase, "we are the last Bulongic," oft repeated during these interactions, is particularly interesting to analyze; it should be considered in the context of this highly specific configuration of relationships that exists between the older men and the young.

Indeed, a Bulongic would never utter this kind of expression in earnest before an outsider. On the contrary, to identify as Bulongic (or Baga) in a non-Bulongic environment is a source of prestige, given the formidable reputation these secretive coastal peoples enjoy in Guinea today. Yet for an old man to declare before his sons, "We are the last Bulongic" is a way of demonstrating to them their exclusion from possessing knowledge that the old still have. By referring to their initiations and the secrets they involve, carnal moments experienced exclusively within the sacred groves, the initiated elders are alluding to the notion that there is a higher order of truth that the young may not attain. As I mentioned above, during our discussions, I had the impression that the elders were doing all they could to show that there were still secrets, while simultaneously emphasizing the highly dangerous and precious nature of these secrets that they had acquired at the time of custom, and the impossibility of those being transmitted today. In fact, the elders' discourse in regard to their religious past is steeped in metacommunicational implications, something Zempléni calls "secretion" (1976):[10] "Everything is still there, it's dangerous and it has extraordinary ritual potential, but we cannot pass it onto you."

In short, from the perspective of the old men, transmitting anything of the pre-Islamic past is now seen in terms of loss, in stark contrast to our positive, not to mention glorifying, patrimonialist metaphor of the transmission of knowledge. Their refusal to transmit what they know does have very real consequences, however: what little the Bulongic elders choose to say in relation to their experience of the pre-Islamic past shows how little is required to transmit something. They do not need to say much to instill fear and fascination in the young: a few words here and there, some nonverbal allusions, gestures, and body language, all of which are enough to reconstruct a world used as a show of power.

The Feminization of Custom

While men, in the name of Islam, have put an end to their old public ritual performances and initiation practices, locking themselves away in the silence of their secrets, the older women, who also lived the time of custom before 1954, continue to dance and sing. "Today," they say defiantly, "the men aren't interested in custom anymore; it's the women who take care of custom." In addition to the ethnographic research I carried out with the young villagers and initiated elders, what I learned from these old women, who have kept up their pre-Islamic ritual practices to this day, allowed me to note the crucial role they play in the dynamic of religious transmission, a process I call the "feminization of custom."[11]

Among the Bulongic, the women are able to set up an original female ritual experience through their secret association (called *kèkè*). As with many female societies in this subregion, here the group's role is primarily anti-witchcraft and based around collective dancing, during which some of the participants will be possessed. In practice, the women of the *kèkè* are now the last to maintain a ritual house where they carry out ritual practices that most of the initiated elders have now abandoned (consulting invisible entities by throwing kola nuts, putting animals to death for the spirits, etc.). During the course of their dancing, they use traditional instruments and body movements that the initiated elders, in the name of Islam, no longer practice. Only they, the women, continue to sing, mostly in reference to the time of custom, to Mossolo Kombo, to the initiates and their confinement. These are not the secret songs of the sacred grove, to which only the initiated were privy, but rather those that were sung at the time by the women, during the public appearances of the masks, at the end of initiations, or during harvest festivals.

A great number of curious, albeit terrified, children come to watch the women's dances. As they dance and sing, the children and young adults listen, observe, and acquire knowledge.[12] This ability to transmit their culture is something that is never recognized by the initiated elders. While women did have an important role in matters of land inheritance, before it was confiscated by the Guinean government, and while some older men will acknowledge that women play a fundamental part in raising children, one thing is clear: to them, women have nothing to do in the transmission of representations and practices tied to their religious past. And yet, through women's association, not only do they transmit ritual practices and representations to other women in the group; by virtue of being the last Bulongic to carry out any public pre-Islamic rituals, what they do implicitly concerns the entire region.

Urban Elites and Their Sense of Loss

There is one final category of actors that deserves our attention: the city dwellers who have left their villages behind to become part of the new urban elite, though remaining significantly involved in village life. The fact of being educated or part of the urban fabric of Conakry, Kamsar, Boké, or Boffa (maritime Guinea's second cities) has left them with a very particular sense of attachment to their former rituals. Among these urban migrants, there exists today an image of the past quite different from that of the initiated elders and old women of the village, something I attribute to their having acquired international notions of heritage and cultural preservation, concepts stemming directly from our modernity, fond as it is of authenticity and hoarding objects and cultures. Their discourse surrounding the need to transmit their culture is not simply based on a local interaction relating to the possession and transmission of hidden knowledge (as it is among the young men of the village and the elders); it is also linked to a universalist conception of their culture, which, like other cultures, is seen as fragile on a global historical scale. Listening to them, it is for the good of humanity that the "burning libraries" must be preserved and recorded, folkloric dances photographed, and books written, so that their culture may be stored and known.[13]

Whenever he goes back to his village, D. Bangoura, a public official in Conakry, questions the older members of his family about their genealogical past. He tells me that he is researching the past because "our elders could not write," and that "everything is going to disappear." Elsewhere, a resident of Kamsar got together with three fellow migrants to buy a mask for their village in order to preserve Bulongic culture. For these urban dwellers, with their financial and moral support, any event, be it a football match or the inauguration of a new school in the village, is an opportunity to organize the "genuine" Bulongic dance. This kind of attitude is part of a relatively new trend among educated urban migrants of wanting to preserve their cultural heritage in writing, photographs, and videos, and reflect on it. In 1988, Ibrahima Camara wrote a small volume entitled *Traditionalisme Baga*. It was distributed among the villages and in Conakry, and described "our unwavering attachment to this people";[14] to the "veritable libraries of tradition that are its elders";[15] its "customs that are being lost and must be recorded";[16] this "art that is being lost";[17] and these "disappearing Baga dances."[18] All of which is "truly regrettable insofar as the most brilliant elements of Baga civilization are being lost to ruin."[19] In short, "The time has come to attempt to rescue it. . . . Elders, we beg you to speak, for your descendants, for the whole world."[20]

"For the whole world." From one perspective reminiscent of patrimonialists, the urban elites thus lay the emphasis on the definitive loss of the true culture. The problem is the subject of frequent discussion among them, during which each stresses the detrimental impact of this loss. All of them insist on the need to sensitize the initiated village elders, so that they may agree to perform the old dances. In contrast to the elders, the men and women I met in the cities or during their stays in the village speak openly about their ritual past. I was struck by the rich, sometimes autobiographical discourses these urbanites contributed, made up of a thousand anecdotes, and the accumulation of a multitude of details. This reference to the most wonderful elements of their village past is a constant theme, and there is a certain pride in having once been these "indestructible fetishists." According to them, the village space is bursting with places of magical power, ritual experts, hidden objects, and dangers and prohibitions. The topography of the land brings together a veritable ritual geography relating to their religion prior to 1954. "There is something buried in this place that represents 'the strength of the Bulongic'"; "this elder still possesses that very powerful secret"; "this rock leads you underground, straight to the sacred grove"; "this is where only the strong can enter." I could provide many more examples bearing witness to this way of describing the village in direct continuity with this powerful ritual past: "The fetishes, the primary weapons were abandoned, but the elders' techniques remain." Being removed from the village no doubt leaves them with a certain sentimental attachment to this past. Even Mossolo Kombo is now a part of life in Conakry: "The spirit Mossolo Kombo comes to see those of us who moved to Conakry in particular. You recognize him straight away. He goes straight to the children. He picks out the families by their language. He plays with the children. He always carries a cane and raffia. You recognize him immediately." And so the entity that once upon a time presided over the initiation of young boys has now become a spiritual agency with no borders: "Every Bulongic child is followed by Mossolo Kombo. If you go to Europe, he'll follow you. He speaks all the languages." He has become a globalized spirit . . .

What this ethnographic portrait has shown is that, even in the absence of initiation rituals and their masks and sacred groves, there still remain subtle processes of cultural transmission at work, suggesting that Bulongic society, despite having been transformed by fifty years of Islamization, still takes part in this pre-Islamic world. The fact that women think of this as the continuation of custom; that the elders persist in refusing to pass it on; and that the people in the city, with the help of the young, are making efforts to record or revive it—all of this will have an impact on the future of cultural transmission. Here, it is mostly the structure of the secret, which is perpetuated by the ambiguous attitude of the initiates, and it is through this local distribution of knowledge that one must grasp the various discourses surrounding cultural loss. For it seems the impending decline of Baga culture, as announced so apocalyptically by Denise Paulme, never happened. The failed predictions of a generation of ethnologists perhaps? As one Baga chief put it in the 1950s, "The Baga are like a heap of cow dung: dry on the outside, moist on the inside." These peoples remain the inheritors of their religious past, in the absence of the objects now preserved in the museums of the West. Now more than ever, we should reflect on our museumified version of Africa, and how, for better or worse, we are fixing the memories of others in their objects. We must examine this romanticized discourse, colored by a nostalgia for endangered traditional cultures, deemed to have been eroded away by imported religions, modernity, and globalization. In the following chapter, I explore the way in which such patrimonialist nostalgia has been deployed by one institution in particular: UNESCO.

2

UNESCO, Bureaucratic Nostalgia, and Cultural Loss

I have more memories than if I'd lived a thousand years.
—Charles Baudelaire, *Les fleurs du mal*

11:30 P.M. Closing time for the bars and restaurants in Luang Prabang, a tourist town in northern Laos, as mandated by a national curfew. With the drinks having flowed freely and their night all too prematurely at an end, nomadic crowds of tourists set out in search of a venue where the evening can continue. One young Brit pulls aside a Lao waiter in a restaurant that accommodates most of the backpackers in town: "Excuse me, what time does the bar close?" the tourist asks. "11:30," answers the waiter. "Why so early?" the man insists, to which the waiter replies, "It's because we're a World Heritage Site. The people who live here get up very early to make offerings to the monks. But the bowling alley stays open past 11:30 if you want to party."

The Obsession with Heritage

Ubiquitous to the point of obsession, heritage is a hallmark of our time. So many texts have been dedicated to this contemporary frenzy—the uncontrollable accumulation of material heritage items—that there is little need to revisit the idea.[1] The nostalgic trope of disappearing cultures represents the very essence of these policies of preservation. Since the inaugural convention of 1972 on the protection of cultural and natural heritage, bolstered by both the 2001 texts on cultural diversity and the 2003 convention on intangible heritage in particular, this has been an essential motif of UNESCO and its experts. As a complex international organization with a focus on transmission, preservation, persistence, and safeguarding of culture, UNESCO has a considerable hand, whether from its Parisian offices or through its experts on the ground, in spreading nostalgic discourses on cultural loss and how to remedy it, and by listing what ought to be preserved and transmitted (be it a place, an object, a dance, a technique, or a religious form).

In *Penser/Classer*, French writer Georges Perec, great lover of lists, wrote: "In every enumeration there are two contradictory temptations. The first is to list everything, the second is to forget something. The first would like to close off the question once and for all, the second to leave it open. Thus, between the exhaustive and the incomplete, enumeration seems to me to be . . . the very proof of that need to name and to bring together, without which the world ('life') would lack any points of reference for us."[2] This need for lists finds form in the very texture of UNESCO's heritage policies, the scope of which assumes heterotopic qualities.[3] Not only do patrimonial actions serve to create veritable heterotopias, nostalgic spaces where time comes to a standstill, in a world experts and foreign tourists think of as disappearing; there is also something eminently heterotopic in the desire itself to list things (whether material or immaterial). The Great Barrier Reef (listed in Australia, 1981), Auschwitz-Birkenau (Poland, 1979), the Royal Palaces of Abomey (Benin, 1985), Angkor (Cambodia, 1992), shrimp fishing on horseback in Oostduinkerke (Belgium, 2013), Fest Noz (France, 2012), the tango (Argentina, Uruguay, 2009), Chichen Itza (Mexico, 1988), Osun-Osogbo Sacred Grove (Nigeria, 2005): all of these are now part of this "sort of general archive . . . the project of organizing in this way a sort of perpetual and indefinite accumulation of time in an immobile place," as Foucault cogently puts it.[4] A dream comes true marvelously realized by UNESCO's patrimonial actions.

Studying UNESCO

While relations between anthropologists and UNESCO are somewhat ambiguous (some work or have worked for it—Alfred Métraux, for example, and Claude Lévi-Strauss on occasion—whereas others see in it the height of universalist imperialism), some researchers have begun to consider UNESCO's policies seriously, and seek to understand, beyond the symbolic charm it holds for most, what it is precisely this institution of culture boasting almost 200 member states is "doing" to today's world. Chiara Bortolotto, Valdimar Hafstein, Christoph Brumann, Sophia Labadi, Lynn Meskell, and Bjarke Nielsen,[5] have conducted ethnographic studies within UNESCO's offices, as well as analyses of its texts and conventions, which, under their anthropological eye, have themselves become research sites where notions of culture, heritage, loss, and a particular kind of authenticity are deployed. They have explored the concrete bureaucratic workings of an international institution of culture and described it in all its complexities, with the contradictory views on culture and heritage, negotiations between delegations, and conflicts between regional offices; in so doing, they bring to light an organization with an at times "inscrutable character,"[6] significantly more fragmented than one would think.[7]

At the same time, other researchers have sought to understand the effects on the ground of UNESCO's universalist—sometimes ethnocentric—policies,[8] delving into the performative power of UNESCO designation. On this subject they encourage us away from facile criticism of the patrimonial act itself, which, like a taxidermist, seeks to freeze "the adventure of transmission"[9] in order to better understand how heritage recognition creates new social, political, economic, religious, and aesthetic configurations. Of course, UNESCO's recognition of a particular site is never a neutral operation. It often has beneficial effects for the region, especially in more precarious places. The preservation of a site brings increased tourism and economic resources. Many studies have shown that, for the inhabitants of UNESCO heritage sites, particularly in countries of the South, designation is a source of both money and pride, and the people generally see the development of tourism in a positive light. But things are never so simple. With the arrival of UNESCO, friction between local inhabitants, as well as political and regional rivalries, can arise. The price of land shoots up, and socioeconomic inequality grows. There are also cases of residents simply not understanding the sometimes abstract notions surrounding heritage and authenticity, which in itself shows the difficulty in implementing international conservation treaties at the local level. Ultimately, on the ground, UNESCO often suffers a bad reputation. Despite its crucial historical role in the decolonization and support of postcolonial nations across the world, the institution and its patrimonial policies have on occasion been described by its detractors as "neocolonial," the embodiment of Western imperialism.

In this chapter, I pursue this line of thought and describe what I call the UNESCOization of Luang Prabang, an ancient royal town of Laos that was listed as a World Heritage Site in 1995. As such, Luang Prabang is a town where the preservation of the past is now a question of "duty, mission, obligation";[10] a certain patrimonialist nostalgia has become a leitmotif as much for UNESCO experts as for some expatriates in the area, local elites, and numerous tourist operators. In the following pages, I describe how nostalgia in Luang Prabang is deployed, the actors, discourses, and contexts involved, and in particular the forms that patrimonial actions here take. Using this example, I propose overall to demonstrate that, behind the notion of nostalgia are a number of cognitive and emotional investments. For UNESCO's heritage experts, Luang Prabang is a vestige of the past world under threat; for Western tourists, a picturesque Oxford of the East, replete with Buddhist mystique; for some inhabitants, a cursed town because of its royal history; for others, a good business investment; a place of pilgrimage for Buddhists; or a temple for the preservation of Lao femininity: Luang Prabang is a hybrid comprising a plethora of different nostalgic (and non-nostalgic) postures. I then explore the unexpected effects of this heritage designation and the touristic boom that ensued. Indeed, although relations between men have always existed in Laos, Luang Prabang is currently described by residents and tourists as a town in the process of becoming gay. Existing in parallel to the town sanctuarized by UNESCO is another Luang Prabang, the "gay paradise" shocking to many of its inhabitants for its stark contrast to the traditional town of monks and pure women.

The UNESCOization of Luang Prabang

In designating Luang Prabang a World Heritage Site in 1995, UNESCO became part of the town's well-documented complex history.[11] Luang Prabang is an ancient royal town. Its history represents the succession of kings dating back to the fourteenth century, when Fa Ngum established the kingdom of Lan Xang over a territory then occupied by Khmu peoples (one of Laos's ethnic groups). It was here he adopted Therevada Buddhism as the state religion with the erection of the famous Buddha statue (the Phra Bang). Starting in the fifteenth century, Luang Prabang was also the scene of a series of invasions by foreign powers: the Vietnamese, Burmese, Thai, Hui Chinese, and finally the French. It was they who, in agreement with the king, drew Laos's present borders and established a protectorate that lasted until 1953.[12] The establishment of the Lao People's Revolutionary Party during the 1950s and '60s led to the Communist revolution of 1975 and the deposition of King Sisavang Vatthana, as well as the exiling of many of the town's inhabitants, now seen as potential royalists, to Thailand, France, or the United States.

UNESCO's arrival on the scene in 1995 occurred against this complicated historical backdrop, when during its Berlin conference, after a long deliberation process involving many stakeholders both Lao and French, it added the town to its World Heritage List. Soon after, a decentralized cooperation initiative was forged between the towns of Chinon in France and Luang Prabang (following Socialist MP Yves Dauge's decision to aid its preservation). Since then, ties between French preservation institutions and officials in Luang Prabang have been strong. Chinon offers technical expertise and ongoing financial support, which has led, some would say, to the development of a particular style of conservation *à la française* (read: centered mainly around monumental material heritage), summarized by one of my interlocutors, who referred to Luang Prabang as "Luang Paris."

In fact today, under the UNESCO umbrella, there are a multitude of different institutional actors involved in the preservation of the town, from the UNESCO experts in Paris and Bangkok to the architects, engineers, and other culture and tourism consultants based in Luang Prabang (short or long term), who, though not strictly speaking employees of the organization, work in close collaboration with UNESCO through their funding by the French Development Agency (Agence française de développement), the European Commission, and the Asian Bank for Development. Since 1995, their joint mission has been to "ensure the continuing authenticity and value of the site" (to use a UNESCO phrase), in particular through a series of actions inside an area corresponding more or less to the town center. These actions have allowed for a local heritage inventory to be drawn up, consisting of 611 houses to be safeguarded against demolition, mainly so-called traditional houses on stilts and colonial houses built during the French colonial period. Moreover, as a holy town, Luang Prabang is home to thirty-four Buddhist temples, still occupied by monks, which have also been listed, as well as certain natural and aquatic spaces that form an integral part of the townscape. The role of the heritage architects is to advise property owners on the subject of renovation; to supervise new construction inside the protected zone (especially building facades and the architectural materials chosen); to report anything unauthorized; and also, on a more general level, to oversee the foreign investors who lease the houses in the town center and transform them into guesthouses and restaurants. Based on the preservation and restoration of religious and local monuments built before the Second World War, this patrimonial policy is set by Heritage House, a conduit for UNESCO policies coming out of Paris, a national organization made up of Lao architects and foreign (usually French) experts, who oversee the correct implementation of the Safeguarding and Enhancement Plan established in 2000 by French architects. For its part, UNESCO's Bangkok office has launched its own conservation projects in town, focusing on the preservation of its intangible heritage by offering, for example, sculpture training to the monks, so that they can learn to restore their own temples. On this subject, contrary to the monolithic image one may have of UNESCO, the principles of preservation themselves are hotly contested between Bangkok and Paris, the former accusing the latter of not paying enough attention to intangible heritage (and at the same time of being too "franco-français").

Experts and Nostalgia

The heritage experts I met in Paris and Bangkok are distinguished above all by their bureaucratic attitude. Their discourse conveys the institutional nostalgia that is part and parcel of UNESCO's very philosophy, a rhetoric based on the irreversibility of loss and the means to resist it, but unrelated to any lived, personal experience. At its heart lie four main propositions:

1. The town of Luang Prabang is a unique and ancient place, whose authenticity is rooted in its precolonial and colonial past.
2. Its authenticity rests primarily on its charm. Indeed, as one official I met in Paris put it, "Heritage in Luang Prabang, it's the life, the atmosphere, the quietness, the spirit of the place." It has a charm reminiscent of London, whose appeal, in the words of Georges Perec, comes not "from its monuments, which have nothing special, nor from its mediocre perspectives, but from all the rest, the streets, the houses, the shops, the people."[13]
3. Luang Prabang is a fragile place. Rooted in a form of cultural Darwinism inherited from the nostalgia of early anthropologists

(see chapter 3), the experts' alarmist rhetoric focuses on the impending threat looming over this town, a victim of brutal modernization, for some of whom "it is already too late." The introduction to a report published in 2004 was explicitly entitled *Luang Prabang: A Special and Fragile Place*.[14] All the heritage experts share the same fear for this town "losing its character, its soul," and for a Lao culture whose aesthetic genius is under threat from the combined continuous assault of tourism (both Asian and Western) and neoliberal consumerism. As one heritage architect says, "Luang Prabang is losing its culture. There is no more culture here. The people no longer know how to transmit it."

4. Finally, tourism is identified as the foremost threat to the preservation of the site's spirit. The influx of tourists distorts the town's charm, where "you see more tourists than people in the streets." Over the past ten years, countless hotels, resorts, and guesthouses have sprung up, and an ethnic artisanal market has been set up specially for the tourists, while restaurants and massage parlors have flourished along the banks of the Mekong and Nam Khan Rivers. There are many cases of downtown residents renting out their houses to foreign investors and deserting the town center to build themselves comfortable homes in the suburbs of Luang Prabang.

Though colored by the nostalgia of bureaucrats for a place whose daily life they do not experience themselves, this discourse does remain self-aware, to the extent that membership of the bureaucratic club allows.[15] Even the categories of heritage used are contested, such as authenticity, "which should be used cautiously," as one of my interlocutors in the Paris offices admitted to me. The principle of heritage designation is never questioned, however, with UNESCO tirelessly defended as an inoffensive organization, "which has no power. We are not trying to do wrong. We propose something and it's the state governments who decide." Behind all the words and conventions are also some very personal agendas, individual stories, and biographies. Early on, for example, Luang

Prabang was described to me as being one particular official's personal project, a term meant to single him out as the biggest contributor toward its designation as a heritage site. And yet, outside these mechanisms of personal appropriation, the overarching sense I had among the experts I met in UNESCO's offices was one of calm, of distance and detachment, a kind of cold, disembodied expertise.[16]

Experts on the Ground: A Militant Nostalgia

The highly emotive way in which preservation manifests on the ground is something altogether quite different. Indeed, the experts I met in the field put paid to the stereotypical notion that expertise and emotion were mutually exclusive. Engaged to varying degrees in the process of conservation on the ground, possessing a profound historical and cultural knowledge of the region, they deploy the nostalgic theme of the town's disappearing charm but combine it with their life experience in the town, rendering it even more emotionally intense. Some among them have lived in Luang Prabang more than ten years and witnessed firsthand the town's recent transformation. It is they who mobilize in defense of heritage in situ, in a society where the type of awareness that UNESCO has for such things is limited to a few choice individuals. Most of the time, their tone is one of indignation and condemnation. To their minds, Luang Prabang has become "Disneyland," a "zoo"; the preservation of the town is a "catastrophe," a "failure," a "wreck," a "disaster!" The town is a "horror," within which they consider their own work as experts a "never-ending struggle": "We've still managed to keep something more or less authentic here. Luang Prabang is something of a success, but it's a never-ending struggle. I'm like a mercenary here!" For others, though, it is "mission impossible."

The recurring example given to highlight their point is the morning ceremony of almsgiving to the monks (Tak Baad), a religious ritual meant to demonstrate the daily generosity of the town's inhabitants to their monks (the monks pray for the people's merit, and in exchange the people give them food), which tourists and locals alike now attend, turning it into "a tourist circus," "a zoo where the tourists feed the monks like animals," where "the tourist is a predator," as one expert declared. Here, daily life as influenced by tourism only serves to reinforce the sense of inevitable denaturation in the town, the irremediable loss of its ambiance. On the other side, the locals too represent for them a major threat to preserving the spirit of the place. Here we find the classic discrepancy between the expert's gaze and that of the inhabitants,[17] who the former emphatically denounce as "kitsch." For example, the Safeguarding and Enhancement Plan formally prohibits glass panes, recently manufactured windows, flowerpots, the cutting down of trees, gates in front of people's houses, lacquer on wood, and many other things that drive my Lao interlocutors to distraction. At the same time, the residents downtown have a tendency to over-occupy their land (to build guesthouses and restaurants), while local authorities have sold certain listed houses to private investors in direct contravention of UNESCO's regulations. To the field experts, the inhabitants of Luang Prabang are always lacking, "unable to preserve their own heritage." The field experts deny the inhabitants all aesthetic and patrimonial competence, a phenomenon similar to the one described by Michael Herzfeld in Rethemnos.[18]

Needless to say, the attitude displayed by these experts on the ground is antithetical to the stereotypical image of the disembodied expert. A stroll through town will see them running around irritably on construction sites, clashing with tourists for not respecting local codes of behavior, even participating in certain religious rituals. Far from Nathalie Heinich's description of the self-restraint displayed by the researchers of the Inventaire général du patrimoine culturel in France, the experts I found in Luang Prabang are actively and physically engaged. Their nostalgia is rooted in having truly experienced a version of Luang Prabang even before its recognition by UNESCO. As one of them said to me, "We feel nostalgic for the Luang Prabang of old. Look, my old house is a pizzeria now." They feel entitled to complement this nostalgia with a patrimonialist discourse on the need to resist loss that, thanks to their intense emotional and cognitive attachment, makes them crucial mediators in the heritage-making process.

An International Community of Loss

The engagement of expatriates who have lived in Luang Prabang for years is equally emotive, as is that of local intellectuals and members of the diaspora (especially those who have returned to settle in Laos permanently after decades of exile): the adopted nostalgia of French, Canadian, or German expatriates mourning the disappearance of the Luang Prabang they once knew; while the exiles returning to their country lament how much the town has changed since they were last there in 1975, blending a nostalgia for pre-Communist Laos and a patrimonialist conscience acquired abroad. One Lao, living in France but returning periodically to Luang Prabang to invest there, worries that "everything is disappearing. We're losing our culture. Luang Prabang has changed so much since I left. There are guesthouses everywhere. And too many tourists. They just do whatever they want here."

There are indeed many expatriates and members of the diaspora who join voices in condemning the changes that have appeared since UNESCO's designation, upsetting the town's ambiance. Like the experts, they have strong words for the tourism making their town so "squalid," and the associated risk of cultural loss that comes with it. For many of them, Tak Baad has also become the defining metaphor for cultural loss, a powerful lens through which to view how the town is being transformed, with the "shocking" tourists who show up to the almsgiving ceremonies "without knowing a thing about it." And indignation sometimes spills over into physical action. "Yesterday I almost got into a fight with a tourist taking photos of the monks any way he liked," exclaimed one French expatriate, who had lived in Luang Prabang for ten years, and who occasionally goes up to tourists and takes photos of them very close up "to show them just how unpleasant it can be."[19]

On this front, there are a multitude of personal initiatives deployed by local Lao people or expatriates, including campaigns designed to sensitize tourists (particularly to the need for quiet during the almsgiving); a museum educating them about Laos's cultural diversity; and exchange programs featuring international artists. One member of the Lao royal family who has lived in France for twenty years (where he has dabbled in ethnology) has even set up a cultural center from which to showcase regional art; not for tourists, he explains, but rather, "for young Lao to learn about the authentic culture of Luang Prabang, the weaving, the dances, the goldwork, the courtly arts. In my center, we teach the young good manners and correct Lao behavior," adding, "What we're doing here is transmission!" Against anything synthetic, such as fabrics from China or aluminum vases, the director of the center wants to revive old production techniques, something that requires working alongside old artisans from the royal era.

Some officials and local elites share the same concerns regarding conservation, similarly worried about the current extent of tourism, while also stressing the issues affecting educated Lao residents in Luang Prabang. This alludes to the growing influence of Thai culture in Laos (either through television or tourism) and what some have described as France's "colonial" attitude in regard to heritage-building in the town. As one says: "Too many French people work here. Only Lao people should be working in Heritage House." Anxious to safeguard the town's intangible heritage, one of these officials has opened a "children's cultural center" where the town's children learn to play traditional games and musical instruments. All these patrimonial actions are dedicated to Luang Prabang's future, such as centers for cultural preservation and transmission—so long as they do not have too many royalist connotations. As one local official stressed to me, "Now we're starting to revive old rituals, just not those related to royalty. There are some things we don't want back." In short, between the UNESCO experts, the expatriates, the Lao diaspora, and the local elites and officials, we can mark out a transnational community of loss, albeit one defined by a thousand different influences and aspirations, with contrasting cognitive and emotional investments.

Nostalgic Tourists Passing Through

"Les sortilèges de Luang Prabang" (The charms of Luang Prabang): headline of an article published in *Le Figaro* in 2007[20] that describes the ancient royal town of Laos as a "sleeping beauty," a "spellbinding little city," with its Buddhist temples and their promise of serenity, now under threat from growing tourism in the region. In another article published in *Le Monde* entitled "Luang Prabang: Péril au paradis" (Luang Prabang: Trouble in paradise),[21] Bruno Philip laments how, "preyed upon by the predator of mass tourism," the town's very identity is being held hostage, and "runs the risk of paying dearly the price of its success." Rather tactlessly, the journalist goes so far as to compare the current surge of tourists to "a new sack of the town, pillaged in 1773 by the Burmese." Luang Prabang does indeed enjoy an international reputation, and attracts a growing number of Western (Falang) and Asian tourists. According to local statistics from the Office of Tourism, this figure grew from 62,000 tourists in 1997 to 260,000 in 2005. Far from all being motivated by the same nostalgia,[22] tourists come in a variety of different profiles: American backpackers looking for opium, French couples on their honeymoon, British expatriates living in Bangkok, Lao natives from abroad (or other provinces) on holiday, and gay tourists too. Some travelers, mostly the Western backpackers, stop off in Luang Prabang to all get drunk after an exhausting trek "through the jungle." At the same time, the town has become a sexual heterotopia for Westerners and Asians looking for sex with young Lao men. During New Year celebrations, many Lao coming from other provinces arrive in Luang Prabang to anoint their country's most respected Buddhas, while former residents in exile abroad take advantage of the opportunity to visit those members of their family who stayed behind after 1975. For those in exile, Luang Prabang often unleashes a wave of painful nostalgic memories of the time before 1975.

For the majority of tourists passing through, however, Luang Prabang represents a "pretty little traditional town" worth visiting, still shielded from the destructive assaults of modernity, between its French colonial influences and its Buddhist mystique. Most Westerners succumb to the spirit of Indochina that runs through it, plunging tourists into an idealized past, reminiscent for some of Marguerite Duras, with its Indochinese ambiance of old cars, electric fans, bright colors, and wicker furniture. As they walk around town, they like to chat with the monks, an experience described as "charming" and "full of mutual respect" that novices can easily turn to their advantage by getting the tourists' addresses, and often some cash or gifts. Most Westerners stress the authenticity of the place, like one French tourist who declared it a site of "pure humanity"; or the bloggers who wrote: "The town may be a little less peaceful, but the markets and a solid meal for 5,000 kips (0.4 euros!) confirmed for us that Laos still retains its authentic soul." Many do, of course, lament what is being lost as well, like the three Dutch tourists (from my introductory vignette) standing in front of a temple, regretting the fact that the locals no longer wore traditional clothing, yet relieved to have visited the town now ("and not ten years from now"), before modernization and tourism had ruined it all. While the majority of Westerners are concerned for the potential loss of its ambiance, there are many Thai tourists flowing into Luang Prabang seeking an image of Thailand from "fifty or a hundred years ago." For these tourists, the town, just a short trip away, represents a mix of relaxation and fun (hiking through the surrounding area, or taking a speedboat down the Mekong); nostalgic curiosity and exoticism (observing the lives of the Lao, whom they generally consider a backward people, or eating a baguette in the town's French restaurants); and religious experience (making morning offerings to the monks and anointing the town's Buddhas). Asian tourists do not experience the same feeling of enchantment for the Indochinese spirit as Westerners do. However, one does get the impression that, despite the variety of different travelers in Luang Prabang, the pleasure derived from visiting the town is generally based on nostalgia, albeit a sanitized form with newly paved roads, clean guesthouses, and mouthwatering food. For Western tourists as much as Asians, this kind of nostalgia is shaped by a fascination for the spirit of a bygone age, the picturesque glorification of a past blending precolonial religious atmosphere with colonial ambiance. Luang Prabang constitutes a stage for Old World fantasies that are continually reinforced by the tourists themselves, who succumb to this taste for the ancient and the traditional; but also by the tourist operators, and the restaurant and hotel owners (be they French, Thai, Vietnamese, Chinese, Singaporean, or Lao), who peddle this nostalgia for a Laos of old, as something to be consumed, a posture that Peleggi refers to as the "nostalgia business."[23] Fearful for a loss of cultural diversity, combined with a nostalgia for a past that does not belong to them, Western tourists have only a very thin level of attachment to the heritage of Luang Prabang. In their case, there is no mobilization in the name of heritage, and rarely any indignation, merely a passing nostalgia, for some, before being swept up again in the next big touristic adventure.

Discrepancies Surrounding Loss

Leaving behind the nostalgia of experts, heritage-building elites, expatriates, and tourists for a world that has already disappeared, or is disappearing, I now explore what the majority of Luang Prabang's inhabitants think of this imperative to resist loss. Do they too yearn for a past where "there were no traffic jams, if you don't count the bikes," one where "tourists didn't exist" or "the streets were made of dirt?" How do they experience the transformation of their town into a heritage site, and, more importantly, do they actually identify with UNESCO's preservation policies? To answer these questions, I conducted a series of interviews with some of the downtown residents, including guesthouse and restaurant owners, souvenir vendors and market traders, residents who had left downtown for the suburbs and neighboring villages, Heritage House officials and architects, local intellectuals, politicians, and monks and other Buddhist religious figures. Naturally, one should bear in mind the sheer plurality of views here, including those who stand to profit from the town's "museumification" and those who do not; the heritage workers who work for UNESCO; and, of course, the monks.

Ostensibly, however, there do exist certain common perceptions surrounding what constitutes *moladok*, the local term for "heritage." *Moladok* is the word normally used by the people of Luang Prabang to designate family inheritance, to convey the idea of "something that must be preserved and passed on between generations." Since UNESCO's arrival, however, *moladok* has acquired a new meaning, namely, the preservation of buildings, both lay and religious, as well as aquatic spaces for the good of mankind and its future; this idea is clearly not so self-evident for a good number of my interlocutors, for whom the perceived benefits of tourism and its economic implications are of greater importance. The pragmatic residents of Luang Prabang do, however, recognize the intimate connection between heritage and tourism: "If we stop heritage or lose our UNESCO title, then the tourists won't come anymore."

Indeed, a significant majority of the town's inhabitants acknowledge that their lives have very much changed for the better in the past ten years. All show a certain pride at the idea that their town is an internationally recognized destination where tourists come to spend their money. This increase in economic opportunities is the most cited positive impact I hear from my interlocutors, UNESCOization having created many jobs (albeit unequally) both in town and in the countryside, including among guesthouse owners, rickshaw drivers, and producers of ethnic handicrafts. And yet, however much they may profit from the town's museumification, however proud they may be of its international recognition, there are still many who emphasize the new restrictions now weighing on them. The issue of heritage often only comes up in complaint at the strictness of heritage regulations, seen by some as truly hellish (*moladok monahok*, literally, "heritage is hell"). Indeed, more than anything, Heritage House is perceived as an institution designed to prohibit "this or that," and it is this feeling of being so constrained that fires most of my discussions ("*Moladok* is all well and good, but we can't build things the way we want to anymore. The problem is we can't build the way we need to"), given the severity of UNESCO's regulations. Moreover, UNESCO has clearly stirred up feelings of disenfranchisement among the residents, who say that "*moladok* is trying to restrict our property rights. These lands belong to us. We used to be able to repair things however we wanted; now we have to ask permission from Heritage House." Elsewhere, adherence to the *moladok* style has proven limiting for local architects, who are no longer able to develop new forms of architecture, instead having to follow the typologies and use the materials dictated to them by UNESCO's architects; this has created a relative architectural homogeneity downtown (condemned by one Lao architect, who told me that Luang Prabang was "not a town of innovation").

But this sense of institutional restriction is most apparent in the question of *intactness*, of preserving the old as it was before, an idea held very dear by the heritage architects but opposed by the inhabitants of Luang Prabang. Most of my interviewees, who do possess an aesthetic competence, whatever the experts may say, applaud the improvements made to the temples, and some enjoy living in *style ancien*, albeit renovated, wooden houses. On the other hand, they cannot grasp UNESCO's insistence on only wanting to use old materials, materials considered less solid and, crucially, more expensive, something demonstrated by some of the dilapidated houses downtown still lived in by their owners, unable to afford the costs of renovation. As one of my interviewees tells me, "The problem with *moladok* is that they want everything to be preserved in the old style, whereas people here want to be able to make modern modifications. Heritage House is too wrapped up in wanting to do everything like before. We don't have to keep everything." As Grant Evans aptly describes, in Luang Prabang expatriates "swoon over what is left of French colonial architecture, or traditional Lao wooden houses, while the Lao themselves dream only of the new concrete houses designed for the Thai nouveaux riches."[24]

Looking further, these sentiments are rooted in a common discourse of access to modernity that, in the context of Laos, is by no means nostalgic. While the UNESCO experts may yearn for a Luang Prabang of old, most residents do not mourn the disappearance of an idyllic, supposedly better past; in the words of one old man, "Things have changed a lot around here, and that's very good!" "The past is the past," says another. "We have no regrets. Before, it was good, but now it's even better." In fact, local discourses tend to emphasize a desire to see "even more tourists and airplanes coming to Luang Prabang." In this context, UNESCO's recognition is associated more with rapid-pace change than with the desired continuity. And local attitudes toward preservation are seen as a way of stepping into modernity, not away from it, as the experts and tourists would have it. Furthermore, there are many in Luang Prabang who see their heritage-listed downtown with its old houses as a relic to be shown to future generations. People may well support UNESCO's conservation policies "to show our children and grandchildren, but we don't want to live like that."

And local forms of nostalgia are very different from the globalized nostalgia invoked by UNESCO. As mentioned above, the heritage-making agenda comes with risks of cultural disappearance, exemplified by the paradox of UNESCO as a force for both preservation and globalization. One local intellectual protests that "UNESCO is all well and good, but since they've been here, all you see are Westerners out in the streets. Now we're afraid of losing our culture." There are many former exiles returning to Laos today (after thirty years abroad) who mourn the disappearance of the town they knew before 1975. Generally speaking, older people tend to denounce the cultural transformations of today, condemning changes in the way people dress, for example, or women's haircuts, as well as how the young now behave ("they no longer greet each other by joining hands, instead they kiss"). Some miss the sociability and mentality of a previous time ("people have less time for family and friends because there's only business here now"). And the rapid changes brought on by UNESCOization have indeed been a source of concern for the inhabitants about their future. Interestingly, for some, these fears take the form of postcolonial imagination. On multiple occasions in Luang Prabang I heard my interlocutors gossip indignantly about the fact that "UNESCO just wants to build a *meuang Falang* here" (literally a "French town," by extension a "town for Westerners"), like the man claiming, "In ten years, there'll only be *Falang* left. They buy up everything around here." Some even go so far as to see Heritage House as being in cahoots with the foreigners to turn Luang Prabang into this *meuang Falang*, with *moladok* being a new form of French colonization (though others point out that Heritage House's role is in fact to supervise foreign investments in town). Rumor enough to demonstrate the dispossession and uncertainty felt by the residents in this postcolonial context.

The Space of Tradition and Women's Bodies

Another local expression of nostalgia with regard to the changes seen in Luang Prabang comes from common representations of tradition and femininity. In the minds of most Lao people, Luang Prabang is essentially the country's traditional and religious center. But, for the majority of its residents, "tradition" takes on a whole new meaning, far removed from the alternative reality of the developing heritage-scape. In this context, the behavior of women represents a moral benchmark against which to measure tradition and its transmissibility. "Here in Luang Prabang," declared one of my interlocutors proudly, "we respect tradition, while in the capital, Vientiane, it's disappearing." Indeed, the women of Luang Prabang are reputed throughout the country to be the most respectful of tradition. This contrasts with the reputed notorious debauchery not only of Vientiane (where women are corrupted by city life), but also of female tourists, American or Japanese in particular, whose body language, attitude, and dress are deemed wrong, while their sexuality is seen as exuberant and uncontrolled for how they "come here and try to sleep with the monks." These discourses are rooted in the Lao "sex/gender system"[25] that equates women's bodies with respect for tradition, especially in Luang Prabang. Since 1975 and the socialist revolution, the authorities have emphasized the need for women to respect traditions.[26] My older interviewees recall how, before 1975, young women would wear miniskirts and dress "like Americans, which after 1975 we couldn't do anymore." For ideological and economic reasons (especially to reduce imports), the Lao government issued a decree in regard to the *sinh*, a silk item of clothing like a skirt, described as the traditional garment of Lao women, and mandatory in official buildings, schools, and temples. This kind of compulsory dress code is encouraged by many women, for example, one representative of the Laos Women's Union who, in an interview for the *Vientiane Times*, explained how "certain women dress inappropriately, without respect for Lao traditions. This can lead to a number of social problems, such as rape, prostitution, or family conflicts. This tarnishes our national culture as well as the reputation of our women."[27] In Luang Prabang, this piece of silk is metonymically linked to an extremely strict code of femininity that mandates that women, as guarantors of traditions, should speak quietly, always be discreet, do the housework, never express any sexual desire, and, above all, remain chaste until marriage. Despite the common expression that "some of the girls in Luang Prabang are lost" (because they wear jeans, cut their hair, go out alone in the evening, meet up with Westerners, or enjoy sex, all seen as transgressions), and the rumors that spread (about young women having sex before marriage or secret abortions), as a rule, in Luang Prabang, "women should not leave too big a footprint" (a phrase used by one of the women I spoke to). This reference to spatial movement is apt in this case. A "disciplined" and "polite" woman operates within the spatiality between the market in the morning, her home or place of work during the day, and her domestic space in the evening, in front of the television with her parents or husband; and in Luang Prabang, rumor and gossip are effective means of enforcing this behavior.

The annual celebration of Miss Luang Prabang (Nang Sankhaan) is the culmination of this representation of femininity in the public space. The beauty contest is highly revealing of the links that exist between femininity and respect for religious traditions. The winner and her six *dauphines*, reenacting the mythical scene of Phagna Kabilaphom,[28] take pride of place atop a parade float during the religious procession (Hê Vo) that runs through the center of town during the Lao New Year (Pi Mae Lao), and have the honor on this occasion of anointing the most prestigious Buddhas. This mythical scene is revived every year, and is also a showcase for the eminent .moral beauty of the contest winners, who, in addition to their large, dark eyes, long hair, fine faces, and light skin, are purported to be virgins from good families known for their respect for religious traditions. In this gendered regime, the place of men is quite different; they are freer in their spatiality and their sexuality. Whereas for young women marriage is, at least in theory, the condition of access to sexuality, it is acknowledged that young men have a natural excess of sexual desire in need of release, often in secret with prostitutes coming in from the countryside, or with transvestites, in the guesthouses outside town or the toilets of a restaurant. In short, while tourists and UNESCO experts see Luang Prabang as a traditional town to visit and preserve from the destructive onslaught of modernity, it is also a place shackled by tradition and a heteronormative ideological nationalism centered around family and marriage. Here we see the outline of a public space governed by the policing of female and male behaviors, and beholden to heteronormative values of chastity and the enforcement of traditional spatiality, all upheld by female collectives, religious dignitaries (*saathu*), teachers, politicians, local leaders, and family members. Furthermore, some of the people I interviewed were pleased that UNESCO, through its preservation policies, was actually encouraging a form of cultural conservatism through conservation. To one man's mind, "heritage, UNESCO, it's all very good because it means we're holding on to the old ways. For instance, women have to wear the *sinh* to go into the temple. Without UNESCO regulations, the girls would wear pants in the pagoda. Seeing girls in pants, it's not nice, it's not good."

Gay Sexscape and the Eroticization of Luang Prabang

One of the more unexpected effects of UNESCO designation and the resulting tourist boom, despite the fact that relations between men have always existed in Laos, is that Luang Prabang is now described by its inhabitants and tourists as a town going gay, "the gayest place . . . anywhere in the world," as one tourist posted online.[29] On another gay forum, someone writes how "the tourist population seemed to be . . . extremely gay. Everywhere you looked there were gay men, usually middle-aged, usually in couples."[30] In fact, there is another Luang Prabang, the "gay paradise" (a phrase often used by expatriates) that clashes with many of the residents (who tend to be highly critical of it, though not to the point of violence), in stark contrast to the town of tradition with its monks and its pure women.

To begin with, there are many businesses in town owned by gay foreigners (mainly French, Belgian, German, British, and Dutch), some of whom are in relationships with Lao men. There is also the tradition of *kathoey* in Luang Prabang, undoubtedly the most visible sign for a foreign visitor. In Laos, *kathoey* is a generic term for all men who sleep with other men. In a narrower sense, it refers to effeminate transvestites who dress like women and personally feel like women. Most have not undergone surgery, though some do now travel to Thailand for sex changes; for many Lao they represent the structural opposite of femininity, negatively described as flamboyant, shrill, flirtatious, shameless, exhibitionist, unfaithful, and, above all, sex-starved prostitutes who sell themselves to locals, expatriates, and visiting tourists. And yet, through their appearance and behavior, *kathoey* do occupy a visible role in Luang Prabang society, particularly during certain traditional performances (including the Lao New Year parade and the annual boat racing festival along the Mekong, now something of a heritage highlight).

Gay tourism in Luang Prabang has flourished over the past few years.[31] As a result, certain cafés, nightclubs, restaurants, and massage parlors have become cruising spots for gay visitors from America, France, Australia, Thailand, or Japan, who, by their fleeting presence, have turned Luang Prabang into a "sexscape," a space "inextricably tied up with transactional space."[32] Many of the young men from Luang Prabang and the surrounding countryside—especially those working in the town's bars, restaurants, and massage parlors—exchange sex for money with the local expatriates and gay tourists, without themselves being *kathoey*-type transvestites or even defining themselves as gay. Indeed, since 1995, male prostitution between Lao and Westerners has thrived, with its own spaces and temporality—a hotel room, a restaurant bathroom, upstairs in a café. The town's geography shifts according to the time of day: at night (after 10:00 P.M.) and early in the morning (before 5:00 A.M.), before the monks begin to wander the town in search of offerings, and while the locals are still asleep, couples can be seen coming together or going their separate ways, usually Lao boys and Western men. All of this occurs as if, in parallel to the daytime spatiality of heritage life, there existed one of nocturnal encounters between men, featuring the same scenario and the same set of questions tirelessly repeated in English: "What's your name? Do you work here? Do you have a wife? Are you here alone? Do you like boys?"

As a sexual heterotopia for gay expatriates and tourists who see the town as a cruising ground, Luang Prabang is undoubtedly reminiscent of the eroticization of other spaces that for Europeans have long provided the possibility of a sexual world in parallel.[33] And it must be said that this kind of sexualization of bodies and places does continue to dominate the gaze of many Falang visiting Luang Prabang. On the one hand, the town is the scene of a "phantasmatic Indochina,"[34] an ambiance reinforced by the tourists and UNESCO experts, and by the restaurants and hotels all peddling nostalgia for a Laos of old; and on the other hand, it is transformed into an eroticized space in which, to the delight of gay tourists and expatriates, "you dare do what you would never do in Europe." One of my interlocutors, a gay expatriate, summed it up for me: "The guys are super hot around here! They don't do anything with their wives. You know you're meant to fuck your wife as little as possible. But they let themselves go around Westerners. First you fuck, then you talk." Mirroring the drowsy picture of Luang Prabang, home to the most traditional women in Laos, is this gay paradise, with "the hottest guys in the country." Even the town's monks, though subject to vows of abstinence during their retreat, are not excluded from the process of eroticization. Certain tourists describe the bad behavior that occurs among some of them, for example. As one young woman said, "Some of them behave badly. Sometime you see a boy in a club with his head shaved in normal clothes partying with his non-novice friends. Or a novice might have dirty pictures of girls on his phone. . . . Some novices even told me that they watch dirty movies on TV in their temple as soon as their superiors have gone to bed." This sexualization of the monks has its counterpart in the gay heterotopia. For example, a British travel magazine that advertises hotels in Southeast Asia eroticizes the morning almsgiving ceremony, a religious scene that, in the words of the anonymous author, turns into a queer performance of "naughty monks": "Luang Prabang even has three gay bars, which intrigued me. . . . How does such a small town in northern Laos have three gay bars? The answer must lie in its . . . naughty monks. Between midnight and 6 in the morning, some of them throw off their orange robes and break out of their temples to go dancing. And they tiptoe home at 6 A.M. for the morning offerings. This will make you look at the daily parade of monks in a different light. . . . As they walk by you one by one, you can't help but wonder—could he be one of them?"[35]

Sex, Drugs, and UNESCO

Acknowledged by all, though impossible to quantify, the proliferation of sexual relations between men is perceived negatively by many of Luang Prabang's inhabitants as a testament to the rapid changes brought about by the town's UNESCOization since 1995. Contrary to the myth of sexual tolerance in Southeast Asia, generally depicted as a region where people are more tolerant of homosexuality,[36] the locals are by no means in favor of this phenomenon. Most of the residents of Luang Prabang hold the Westerners, more than anyone else, responsible for this evolution. One young man told me, "The *kathoey* come with the Westerners. You're the ones who like *kathoey*. So they follow you!" Another man I interviewed explained how "sleeping with a Falang brings money for the whole family. Often the parents let it happen. The *kathoey* are rich around here"—a notion readily expressed by the common refrain "boys here are worth gold" (*pusae mi kham dju ni*), used to describe male prostitution with Westerners as a means to earn money for oneself and one's family. Some inhabitants directly blame the French members of UNESCO, who have made this town a patrimonial heterotopia, a source of great benefits, and a destination for male prostitution; according to one, "Heritage is to blame, UNESCO. Before, there were two or three *kathoey* here; now there are many. It's the old French director, when he worked at Heritage House, who brought all his *kathoey* friends over. That's why there are so many of them now." Similarly, there are many educated Lao who point to the harmful influence of Thai culture, which, through television, has made *kathoey* lifestyle acceptable and even desirable. Indeed, the *kathoey* are accused of coming from elsewhere, mainly Thailand. Following the old rhetorical line painting homosexuality as a foreign import, this gay paradise is never described as a Lao creation; it is Thai or Western.[37]

It is interesting to note overall that the residents of Luang Prabang who lament the passage of time are not mourning the irreversible disappearance of the houses, temples, and traditional rituals that UNESCO experts seek to preserve. I was struck by the relative lack of complaints, from young and old alike, regarding the transformation of Tak Baad, the dawn ritual of almsgiving. There are, of course, older people and heritage elites, as well as certain religious leaders (*saathu*) whose temples stand in the main tourist zone, who are rightly concerned to see Tak Baad essentially becoming dependent on the tourists and foreigners who live in these areas that have been abandoned by their former inhabitants. As mentioned above, Tak Baad has also been appropriated gradually as a symbol of loss by recent campaigns (mainly organized by expatriates). Most residents, however, insist that they are maintaining tradition. For one woman, "customs don't disappear, not even with tourism. Lao people preserve their traditions. Tak Baad won't disappear. It's a Lao tradition." According to one old man, "Even if people do rent out their houses and leave town, I'm not worried.

Even with the Falang, Lao tradition will survive. Besides, the Falang are actually helping us to preserve Tak Baad." To which I could add a great many more examples.

What my ethnographic research in Luang Prabang demonstrates is the existence of a common discourse that ties together heritage, postcolonialism, the West, moral decline, and gay peril. While Luang Prabang's touristic development, under the aegis of UNESCO and the Lao government, rests on the image of a holy town, one of temples and monastic processions, it is also contributing to the creation of a gay paradise. Though this involves two seemingly incompatible sides of Luang Prabang, it reflects the very paradox at the heart of UNESCO and the international heritage mission. Here is an institution whose policies seek to preserve both places (since the Convention of 1972) and cultural practices (since the Convention of 2003), but which also produce a dynamic effect on the very places and practices they aim to protect. Making Luang Prabang into a sanctuary to be guarded by UNESCO against destruction is also exposing it to the effects of tourism, to a transformation with wide-ranging and ill-defined parameters: a place henceforth open to foreign capital; the spread of multiple categories of actors with contrasting visions (whether expatriates or tourists and their exotic/erotic desires); the proliferation of encounters between diverse groups of people (Lao, Falang); and the formation of new identities, most notably in terms of sexuality and gender. While for most of the town's inhabitants, these changes fuel rhetoric of collective danger and moral peril tied to the West, modernity, heritage, and homosexuality, they also serve to define Luang Prabang's place in a globalizing world.

Exonostalgia/Endonostalgia

To conclude this chapter, I want to delve further into the workings of nostalgia. Grant Evans[38] and, more recently, Colin Long and Jonathan Sweet have demonstrated how UNESCO's recognition of Luang Prabang is based on a nostalgic "quest for an Idealized, Orientalized 'real Asia.'"[39] However, claiming that there exists a single nostalgic posture is problematic. Here, I would like to refine this proposal, by highlighting the protean nature of the nostalgic attachments and the emotional and cognitive investments at stake in Luang Prabang. First of all, in order to clarify a theoretical situation that strikes me as too vague, I propose a distinction between two nostalgic postures: nostalgia for a past that has been experienced personally (*endonostalgia*); and secondhand (or vicarious) nostalgia, *exonostalgia*, characteristic of Western tourists and Paris-based experts. The former involves a personal ownership of the past, Proust's famous madeleine being the most emblematic reference of this kind of experience. The latter refers to nostalgia for a past that one has not personally lived, entailing feelings of loss that are detached from the direct experience of loss.

On this basis, Luang Prabang can be considered an arena for the deployment of different types of nostalgia. First, there is the bureaucratic nostalgia of the experts based in Paris and Bangkok, exonostalgia characterized by a generalist discourse on loss. Second, there is the entitled nostalgia of the experts in situ, an exonostalgic discourse rooted in profound historical and cultural knowledge (nostalgia for a culture that is not their own, for a past belonging to others who do not realize what they are losing), combined with an endonostalgic sense for the disappearing charm of a town they themselves have known. The cognitive and emotional attachment is very strong, and in this scenario the expert becomes a militant. The endonostalgia of expatriates, for its part, rests on experience and an intense emotional attachment to "their" Luang Prabang of old, whereas the diaspora Lao, born in Luang Prabang and then exiled, endonostalgically mourn the disappearance of the town of their childhoods (reinforced by a patrimonial discourse developed abroad). Then there is the exonostalgia of tourists, whose own externalist discourse on cultural loss relates neither to their own historical past nor to their culture, and that, in keeping with the very nature of tourism, produces no engagement. Finally, there are the varying forms of nostalgia belonging to the ordinary inhabitants of the town, sometimes royalist in nature, sometimes the feeling of having lost certain values, but lacking the alarmist discourse on the need to preserve heritage and culture, except for the tourism benefits that they get out of it. Of course, endo- and exonostalgia are not mutually exclusive postures. Certain experiences do mix the two, such as the nostalgia felt by the experts on the ground. The endonostalgia of expatriates, an emotional attachment to "their" Luang Prabang of old, is very similar in many ways to the endonostalgia of the Lao diaspora. And is the nostalgia of a European tourist wanting to bring his children to Luang Prabang, as his parents once did, an endo- or exonostalgia experience? Going forward, my proposed typology will have to be refined, but it does prove apt for marking the distinction between different feelings and discourses on loss.

Above all, these nostalgic postures demonstrate specific forms of engaging with the future. Far from being a synonym for *passéisme*, nostalgia serves to reveal existing relations among the past, the present, and the future. Following the historian Koselleck,[40] discourses and feelings on the passage of time should be treated as *always already* framed in the horizons of expectations in the present. The nostalgias of Parisian experts and international tourists are intimately connected, bearing witness to their desire to imagine another world in Luang Prabang, a world capable of resisting cultural homogenization and preserving ethnic diversity. While the latter's horizon is crafted in universalist terms, the same cannot be said for the experts and expatriates living in Luang Prabang, nor for the Lao diaspora whose royalist nostalgia conveys their dreams of potential political changes in particular. And while many of the residents of Luang Prabang are concerned with the current transformation of their towns at the hands of Westerners, a world from which they feel dispossessed, some do cling to hope, like one old man who declared, "Who will remember UNESCO in a thousand years? Laos and Buddhism will still be there, but who will remember UNESCO?" Truly, hope is never far from nostalgia.

In short, Luang Prabang constitutes a *nostalgiascape*. UNESCO experts, foreign tourists, expatriates, and Lao elites of the diaspora all share a nostalgia for a bygone age (whether theirs or not) that glorifies the Indochinese past, an image similarly used by tourist companies and local private investors, and beneficial for the further development of tourism, a crucial factor for most of the town's inhabitants. Whether it is bureaucratic, lived, or consumerist, this nostalgia has very real effects on the urban landscape of the town. Since its designation as a heritage site, many of the houses have been rented out to members of the international cosmopolitan class, affluent types from Singapore, Thailand, France, and Australia, who open restaurants and hotels in the Indochinese style. This nostalgic gentrification that peddles nostalgia to tourists comes primarily from these foreigners, who see Luang Prabang as a charming place to live and a good investment. Evidently, even a heritage setting like this is not immune to the logic of international capital, which is serving to transform the town into an object of consumption, marketed on the basis of its international uniqueness.

Yet patrimonial and consumerist nostalgias are not enough to explain the transformation of Luang Prabang into what it is today. Petra Rethmann has shown how, in post-Soviet Russia, the expression of nostalgia has been made possible by a policy of de-ideologization.[41] In her view, in Moscow, the development of capitalist consumerism has allowed for the emergence of nonsubversive nostalgias. In Laos too, UNESCOization and the existence of a transnational community of loss should be considered concomitantly with the development of capitalist consumerism. They converge with national political needs that are themselves in no way nostalgic. As Sweet and Long have rightly noted, the colonial past, the traditional houses, and the rites that UNESCO helps to preserve are intimately tied to the town's royal history. Grant Evans also reminds us that, in 1975, the revolutionaries immediately transformed the royal palace into a museum with the intent of depoliticizing it and keeping its past under their control.[42] Furthermore, the nostalgic museumification of Luang Prabang should not make us forget that heritage-building serves, in some cases (and particularly for the Lao government), to anesthetize the past and render it harmless to the present. It was Daniel Fabre who stated correctly that UNESCO's mission of recognition "emphasizes above all how much that which is commonly designated 'culture' today has become an idealized, or imaginary, version of the political."[43] In this case, diagnoses of loss and cultural preservation are revealed in all their complexity at a crossroads of nationalist projects, local aspirations for prosperity, the effects of globalization, colonial heritage, and the deployment of multiple nostalgias.

3
Toward the End of Societies?

The old line ethnologist is in the seventh heaven if he can
find a group which has never seen a white man before and he
views the current opening up of the far corners of the earth with
all the alarm of any craftsman whose livelihood is threatened.
—Ralph Linton, *The Science of Man in the World Crisis*

In 1922, anthropologist Bronislaw Malinowski, one of the founding fathers of the discipline of anthropology, who brought the Trobriand Islands in Papua New Guinea to the world's attention,
wrote these now famous words: "Ethnology is in the sadly ludi-
crous, not to say tragic, position, that at the very moment when it
begins to put its workshop in order, to forge its proper tools, to start
ready for work on its appointed task, the material of its study melts
away with hopeless rapidity. Just now, when the methods and aims
of scientific field ethnology have taken shape, when men fully
trained for the work have begun to travel into savage countries and
study their inhabitants, these die away under our very eyes."[1] A
whole century has passed since these pre-apocalyptic lines were
written down. Tracing his footsteps, Australian anthropologist
Michelle MacCarthy traveled to the very place where Malinowski
had predicted this end of worlds, only to report that "while there
have been some obvious cosmetic material changes—such as the
use of Western clothes instead of grass skirts and tapa cloth and

the use of aluminum cooking pots instead of clay pots . . . —many aspects of life—gardening, the use of magic, feasting and village activities—continue more or less *makala tukanibogwa, makala bestuta* (as in the past, so it is today)."² Susan Kuehling, a German researcher who has worked in this region since the 1990s, has also confirmed the vitality of the *kula*, the famous ceremonial exchange system, even if today it has been transformed by the global economy.³

A similar catastrophist perspective can be found in the work of Denise Paulme, the French anthropologist who conducted the first ethnographic research into the Bulongic people during the 1950s. As seen in the first chapter of this book, having done my own investigations in the field fifty years after Denise Paulme, I came to realize how wrong she had been about their imminent disappearance, which in fact never materialized. A diagnostic error, perhaps? The failed prophecies of an entire generation of ethnologists? Were the changes Malinowski and Paulme witnessed then in the Trobriands and among the Bulongic merely cosmetic? This is by no means to deny the traumatic experience and massive social and cultural upheaval felt by so many of the colonized peoples that anthropologists were studying at the time. In most cases, colonialism opened up a "space of death."⁴ From the ethnocide perpetrated against the Amerindian peoples of South America and the United States, to the brutal colonization of aboriginal Australians or the indigenous populations of Congo under Leopold II of Belgium,⁵ the list of traumatized groups runs long. Often enough they were simply exterminated, cultures simply wiped out for good. And yet anthropologists also came to realize, correctly, that the societies in which they worked were enduring, often transformed and syncretic, through their suffering and trauma. Without wishing to fall into a naïve and overly optimistic discourse on the resistance of societies, it must be said that a great number of human groups once thought so fragile have not in fact been wiped out by the—generally brutal—onslaught of modernity, colonization, and globalization. Their cultures have not necessarily been eroded away. In fact, some diagnoses of cultural loss have even proved completely incorrect. In this chapter, I explore this concept of loss, an essential component of anthropology itself, and something we might call a form of disciplinary exonostalgia. Of course, the landscape of anthropology has always been diverse and fragmented. Multiple paradigmatic orientations have emerged from within the same national traditions,[6] and I do not claim to be exhaustive on this topic. Yet rarely were the first anthropologists able to truly extricate themselves from the trope of cultural disappearance.

The Nostalgic Anthropologist

Holly High suggested the existence of a "disciplinary melancholia" in anthropology.[7] Referring to the experience of mourning of one of her main Lao interlocutors, Suaay, High invites us to pay particular attention to the feeling of guilt that can take hold of ethnologists when they return from the field. With the field behind them, some researchers have a sense of having abandoned their interlocutors (especially if they live far away). Postcolonial studies and postmodern critiques have certainly contributed to the development of such feelings of guilt, together with other moral concerns, as Marcus and Fischer themselves attested to.[8] This melancholy seems to be a fairly recent phenomenon, and I believe it is rooted in the ethical need for reciprocity that many researchers now hope for.[9] However, if there is one discursive and emotional posture that has defined anthropology since its beginnings, it is undoubtedly nostalgia.

As highlighted through the ethnographic case in the previous chapter, nostalgia can take many different cognitive and emotional forms. To avoid it becoming a catchall term to label any feeling of regret for the past,[10] and following the efforts made to bring it into clearer focus,[11] I propose to distinguish between exo- and endonostalgia. The former allows us to look at nostalgia as a particular feeling in regard to the past, where the old is glorified and considered lost forever, without necessarily being based on firsthand experience of the time or place. This vicarious nostalgia is particularly applicable to the perspectives of the discipline's founders. Without doubt, many anthropologists have nostalgic memories of their fieldwork. Ethnographic research is a cauldron for endonostalgia relating to intense social events and encounters, but also for the banalities of daily life as lived by the researcher on the ground. We will not be dealing with this kind of nostalgia here. In this chapter, I will focus on a specific emotional and cognitive posture that is engaged in the production of anthropological knowledge, the exonostalgia of the first anthropologists who readily and frequently invoked the "paradigm of the last."[12] At the time, British anthropologist Audrey Richards (who conducted her first fieldwork during the 1930s in Zambia under Malinowski's tutelage) admitted in an interview with Jack Goody[13] that doctoral students of anthropology were going into the field primed to believe that it was already "too late." Witnesses to the end of eras, their ethnographies quickly became cultural obituaries.[14]

There are several points here worthy of discussion, in particular the representations surrounding those societies we used to call "primitive" or "traditional." First of all, for the majority of the founding fathers of this discipline, cultural transmission was a process that supposedly went without saying. Marcel Mauss attests to this idea when he writes that archaic societies "live in a way that is so well adapted to their internal and external milieu that they only need one thing: to continue what they have always done,"[15] and that therefore "the transmission of things and practices, and of collective representations, goes smoothly."[16] In *Primitive Mentality*, Lucien Lévy-Bruhl underlines how, in inferior societies, "the supreme conduct of life . . . is to do what ancestors have done, and to do that only."[17] Adherence to custom is therefore instinctive: the "conservative dispositions" of the primitive man, demonstrated, according to sociologist Herbert Spencer, by their "fixity of habit."[18] In these societies, cultural transmission occurs with minimal difficulty, the last, as Lévi-Strauss later wrote, to be able to do what we ourselves no longer can, namely, "how to smoothly transmit our culture over generations."[19]

Self-sustaining and conservative, traditional societies were considered fragile entities above all, with little ability to withstand transformations. To read most of the sociologists and anthropologists of the early twentieth century, these societies were simply not ready to meet the changes that contact situations incurred. As Lévy-Bruhl wrote:

> Primitive peoples, as a rule, show themselves hostile to everything coming from without, at least unless it be from neighboring tribes like their own, people of the same race, customs, and institutions, with whom they could live on friendly terms. From the real 'stranger' they neither borrow nor accept anything. . . . They form, as it were, sealed systems in which every entrant runs the risk of setting up a process of decomposition. They are like organisms capable of living for a very long time whilst the general environment changes but slightly, but which very rapidly degenerate and die when invaded by new elements.[20]

"Misoneist" societies, with an "aversion to change," they are unable to withstand colonial contact with the whites, seen as the very trigger of their extinction. In this regard, Lévy-Bruhl points out that "intercourse with white people nearly everywhere (North and South America, Polynesia, Melanesia, etc.) has proved fatal to native races. Most of them, decimated by the diseases the whites bring with them, have disappeared, and many of those now remaining are becoming extinct. . . . The primitives' institutions, like their languages, quickly disappear, as soon as they have to submit to the presence and influence of white races."[21] As a result, "In a very short time the native, abruptly exposed to fresh influences, comes to despise and forget his own traditions. His own code of morality tends to disappear, . . . the sense of solidarity of the group is weakened and with it its desire to exist."[22] The aftermath of colonization allegedly saw the end of the authenticity of traditional societies. At best, one might hope to observe a few traces of their past, the odd cultural crumb . . .

At the time, the paradigm of the last was not a French exception. As noted in the introduction to this chapter, in treating the Trobriand islanders as an endangered society from the outset,

Malinowski undoubtedly left himself unable to consider their cultural changes without reducing them to an inexorable weakening of their culture.[23] Similarly, E. E. Evans-Pritchard insisted that "another reason, and very cogent, for studying primitive societies at the present time is that they are rapidly being transformed and must be studied soon or never,"[24] while Raymond Firth presented *The Work of the Gods in Tikopia* as a book that "describes a vanished past, a set of institutions not known to many of the young Tikopia themselves."[25]

For the American perspective, it is enough to read about Theodora Kroeber's Ishi, described as the last Indian savage in North America, the last trace of a Neolithic society exterminated by the whites. And on the subject of Native Americans, Edward Sapir, Boas's own brilliant student, laments how

> when the political integrity of his tribe is destroyed by contact with the whites and the old cultural values cease to have the atmosphere needed for their continued vitality, the Indian finds himself in a state of bewildered vacuity. Even if he succeeds in making a fairly satisfactory compromise with his new environment, in making what his well-wishers consider great progress towards enlightenment, he is apt to retain an uneasy sense of the loss of some vague and great good, some state of mind that he would be hard put to it to define, but which gave him courage and joy that latter-day prosperity never quite seems to have regained for him. What has happened is that he has slipped out of the warm embrace of a culture into the cold air of fragmentary existence. What is sad about the passing of the Indian is not the depletion of his numbers by disease nor even the contempt that is too often meted out to him in his life on the reservation, it is the fading away of genuine cultures, built though they were out of the materials of a low order sophistication.[26]

Here, Sapir's exonostalgia intertwines with that of his interlocutors, who have been exterminated by the American colonists.

In most of these founding texts, the style, condemning the ravages of colonization and globalization, is pre-apocalyptic. There is an evolutionist temporality that pervades their words.[27] In particular, in the works of Malinowski, Boas, or Marcel Griaule, the position of the anthropologist in the narrative is that of a powerless observer, the herald of impending cultural disaster. While these peoples were perceived as the last survivors of a bygone age, the anthropologist became the last witness to these paradises being led inexorably toward their doom. I am particularly fond of Ramon Sarró's likening of ethnography to "the art of being late"[28] to describe the disappointment felt by the first anthropologists arriving in the field just as traditional systems appeared to be crumbling; they were arriving too late.

This feeling of arriving too late is reminiscent of Vladimir Jankélévitch's fine words on the "complacency to the irreversible,"[29] this "impotency before the inevitable."[30] When resisting the irreversible becomes impossible, these two words alone express the "bitterness of regret."[31] Like a doctor watching a patient in agony, the nostalgist feels powerless before the passage of time, as was the case for many anthropologists. Some of them felt outrage and a sense, no doubt, of personal loss. They took to politics to advocate for these peoples, to fight against the prevailing discourse that traditional societies had always been savage and had nothing to offer the modern world. For them, the trope of the "disappearing savage" constituted a political allegory intended to garner public recognition for these groups, a posture of militant exonostalgia. Other anthropologists developed a discursive interest for an object they believed to be in decline, without necessarily expressing strong feelings of nostalgia. However, militant or not, this exonostalgia fueled their scientific activities; they began to archive and collect ethnographic data (referred to by some as "salvage ethnography"). Simultaneously a fear of loss and a theoretical perspective, this exonostalgia very quickly became institutional practice in university faculties, becoming embodied in the collections of objects of museums,[32] to the point of nowadays being deployed by UNESCO experts.

Nonetheless, little by little, anthropologists have abandoned their lament on the disappearance of authentic otherness, replacing it instead with a discourse on the "extraordinary ability of societies to resist erosion."[33] Fragility versus resistance. From the 1930s and '40s onward, anthropologists came to realize that the societies in which they worked were enduring, albeit transformed. The current refrain now states that "cultures do not die, they change." This reminds me in particular of Melville Herskovits, the American anthropologist based at Northwestern University and a student of Boas, who, starting in the early 1930s, developed a pronounced interest in cultural transmission as manifested through the process of acculturation.[34] Although Herskovits had presented himself above all as a thinker on dynamism and contact between cultures, emphasizing the need to consider cultural stability and change together, his insistence on demonstrating the existence of continuities, "retentions," between black cultures in Africa and the Americas is significant. On this subject, Stefania Capone correctly reminds us that Herskovits's *Myth of the Negro* "dealt with the way in which African Americans have preserved their culture in spite of the oppression and discrimination of whites,"[35] with those cultural traits preserved beyond the Atlantic, albeit adapted to their new setting. In so doing, Herskovits foresaw the development of an entire field of research dedicated to their survival in the Americas, the memory of African slaves, and the transatlantic cultural heritage embedded in the present of their descendants, whether American, Brazilian, or Cuban. In advocating a decidedly historicist epistemological posture, he encouraged us more than anything to explore this past and the influence it continues to have on the present of groups and individuals.

In the same vein, Roger Bastide, himself a voracious reader of Maurice Halbwachs and Lévi-Strauss, demonstrated his interest in these "centers of continuity and social conservation,"[36] particularly through "these initiates [who] carried the ethnic gods and ancestors from Africa to America in a physical setting—the intimacy of their muscles—in such a way that in the new land all that was needed for Africa to reawaken and express itself once again, was for them to hear once more the musical leitmotifs of the divinities that they embodied in their flesh."[37] For both these authors, "transmission," which also refers to the circulation and geographic spread of cultural traits across oceans, is synonymous with the persistence of the past into the present. For if culture and traditions continue to be transmitted to this day, this means that they endure in the face of societal changes and sometimes traumatic historical ruptures, a notion that has gained traction in the anthropological community, as we shall see.

Overall, since the 1930s in the United States (and a little later in France with Georges Balandier), nostalgia for disappearing paradises has given way to a discourse on the processes of acculturation, incorporation, and the reinterpretation of new cultural elements, but also the resistance to change and the persistence of "indigenous" elements. In Britain, the same anti-nostalgic perspective was adopted by anthropologists of urbanization and modernization (in the vein of Max Gluckmann and the Manchester School), in a break with old notions of fragility and decline. This recognition paved the way for serious anthropological studies on local perceptions of temporality and cultural changes, often bringing to light the absence of nostalgia in local populations.

Beyond regional traditions, most contemporary anthropologies (be they French, American, or British) are now heirs to these continuist, historicist postures that, freed from the nostalgic trope of disappearance, have opened the door to a veritable cult of persistence—a cult attested to by the first subtitle of Christian Højbjerg's book *Resisting State Iconoclasm among the Loma of Guinea: Things Do Not Always Fall Apart*;[38] like, among others, the rites he observed among the Loma in the region of Forest Guinea, previously the target of repeated iconoclastic campaigns launched by the postindependence government, and which have nonetheless survived until this day. On a similar note, Bruce Knauft remarks how in Melanesia, beyond the tensions born out of postcolonialism, "indigenous practices and indigenous beliefs are far from dead; indeed they resurface with creative regularity,"[39] pointing out the "practical ways in which people find continuities and creative spaces as they engage the possibilities and constraints of change."[40] To which I could add multiple similar examples, such as the persistence of Marrano memory in the Northeast region of Brazil,[41] or of colonial memory during Hauka possession séances in Niger.[42]

Indeed, cultural persistence today can be found under a host of different names, including "resistance studies or the study of post-colonial modernity, ethnicity, syncretism and religious resurgence,"[43] and studies on memories too, which, highlighting their intrinsically transmissible nature, revolve around the question of persistence.[44] Consider, for instance, *Memories of the Slave Trade* by Rosalind Shaw, about contemporary memories of slavery among the Temne people of Sierra Leone. In her book, the author seeks to demonstrate that the Atlantic slave trade has been forgotten in explicit, verbalized terms (for who is left to actually remember it?), but it has still been *implicitly* memorized through the intervention of spirits, landscapes, divination, or witchcraft, or in postcolonial political life. As Shaw sets out in her concluding remarks, "Four centuries of slave trade have neither been erased from memory nor insulated from critical moral scrutiny. . . . In the Temne-speaking communities I knew in Sierra Leone, the slave-trading past was vividly . . . present in such practical forms of remembering as spirits of landscape, diviner's tutelary spirits, ritual protection, divinatory images, stereotypes of wives as channels of incursion, practices of witch-finding, images of the witch-city, stories of human leopards, and rumors of sinister ritual ties between politicians and diviners."[45] What the author describes in her work is the endurance of mnemonic traces of the Atlantic trade in the contemporary interpretative landscape of Sierra Leone; for her, "it became clear that the slave-trading past was not over."[46] Traces of the traumatic past surrounding slavery have been transmitted, albeit concealed and transformed, the result of which is not only cultural persistence, but the persistence of historical trauma into modernity.

It is the same fascination with what is left of the past in the present that pervades the excellent *The Weight of the Past* by Michael Lambek, the Canadian anthropologist who has written extensively on memory.[47] His intention is to describe how "the ancestral past permeates present-day Mahajanga and its environs";[48] how, while the Mayotte town he is studying appears to have been completely absorbed by modernity, "behind gates and fences, in groves on the outskirts and in the distant countryside, at night, in cupboards, in tombs and under wraps, in embodied practices and in the moral imagination, lies the past—all the more powerful for remaining discreetly concealed and protected; set apart but immanent"[49]—a quotation that reveals our author's ambition: to show that, beyond loss and rupture, a coherent cultural system survives, "a set of practices that continue to produce a coherent, polyvalent, and insightful way of comprehending and engaging social change."[50]

For these authors, "memory" is synonymous with *societal* memory in particular, that is, the ability of a society or a culture to perpetuate itself coherently across time, its endurance in fragmented contemporary worlds while preserving within it the mnemonic traces of disruptive events from its past. In other words, memory here means that the past does not evaporate, and that anthropologists are tasked with observing the *continuity* of representations, practices, emotions, and institutions, despite sometimes radical societal changes, whether the effects of, among others, colonialism, globalization, creolization, migration, urbanization, industrialization, socialism, and so on.

Transmission into fragmented worlds, continuity through change, to be sure. This brings to mind the notion of "structure of the conjuncture" coined by Marshall Sahlins,[51] which allows us to reflect how people are able to reproduce their cultures while transforming them; but also continuity in forgetting, in silence. In fact, while memories, gestures, words, emotions, and institutions are all successfully transmitted beyond the vicissitudes of modernity, it now seems clear that the act of forgetting too is passed on, as shown by Janet Carsten among the Malay on the island of Langkawi.[52] Here forgetting has become necessary to the persistence of migrant identities, which are rooted not in the existence of elaborate inherited memories, but rather on the basis of the need to forget their old ties to create kinship relations with new migrants. Ultimately, these are questions of cultural continuity, tenacity, and transmissibility, the tectonic plates on which such debates hinge. For forgetting, ruptures, disjunctions, traumas, and catastrophes represent a lens through which today's anthropologists may consider the endurance of social and cultural systems within the contemporary worlds that they explore. To clarify, memory, resurgence, resistance, reinvention, resilience, reproduction, heritage, persistence, syncretism, habitus, mythopraxis, and other such fashionable contemporary neo-traditionalisms are all terms that, unsurprisingly, relate back to the questions of cultural transmission and its persistence. As Arjun Appadurai cogently states, "In one way or another, anthropology remains preoccupied with the logic of reproduction, the force of custom, the dynamics of memory, the persistence of habitus, the glacial movement of the everyday, and the cunning of tradition in the social life of even the most modern movements and communities, such as those of scientists, refugees, migrants, evangelists, and movie icons."[53] We are no longer tasked with mourning the disappearance of traditional societies. On the contrary, we should be reassured by their capacity to preserve themselves, transformed, at times revitalized, within a postcolonial modernity.

Exonostalgia Is Not (Quite) What It Used to Be

And yet it cannot be denied that the exonostalgic disposition of early anthropology still lingers to this day, sometimes under a different guise, sometimes residually. There are many ways to be exonostalgic nowadays; I do not want to give the impression that all ethnologists express it the same way. Perhaps we should distinguish between those who do and do not succumb to exonostalgia, as in life, where some regret more than others the passage of time. As an example, I remember Luc de Heusch, professor of anthropology at the Free University of Brussels, who up until his death lamented the paradigmatic shifts occurring within our discipline. De Heusch believed that, through modernization, anthropology had lost its traditional objects of study (primarily societies without writing), similarly to his mentor Lévi-Strauss. There are still some anthropologists who prefer to focus on so-called nonindustrial societies, lured by the exploration of the exotic under threat. Terre Humaine, the French book series founded by Jean Malaurie in 1954, is emblematic of this, having published a great number of monographs condemning the ravages of loss and cultural extermination, urgently seeking to preserve the memories of endangered populations. Even if Pierre Aurégan encourages a more nuanced reading, it is hard not to see in it "a lengthy plea, full of nostalgia and pathos for endangered minorities and cultures."[54] Similarly, there are still certain colleagues working for UNESCO or other international conservation agencies who exhibit a rhetoric based on patrimonial exonostalgia. However, in the West, the invocation of this kind of nostalgic trope is today met with little enthusiasm. In many cases, anthropological nostalgia "isn't what it used to be."[55]

First of all, if nostalgia is not what it used to be, there are still expressions of exonostalgia among today's anthropologists in their chosen fields of study. There is no doubt that anthropologists still have their favorite others. Empathic identification, the founding principle of our discipline (which I will explore further in the next chapter), does not work in the same way with regard to all the categories of actors one encounters in the field. Although ethnological otherness enjoys a broader definition today than in the past (including as it does Wall Street traders, Chinese entrepreneurs, university-educated Aborigines, or UNESCO experts, among others), there are many researchers who exhibit sentimentality for the "local." Along with the "remote" so well analyzed by Ardener,[56] "local" (by which we mean local populations, local actors, local practices) is a complex and emotionally loaded notion that has come to replace the term "indigenous," but wherein similar ideas of cultural and social particularism and heterogeneity converge. I do not think it is far-fetched to say that a number of today's anthropologists have "nostalgified" what is local, particular, and heterogeneous. A few comments on my own research in Luang Prabang, in northern Laos, should suffice to clarify my position. As demonstrated in my second chapter, the town of Luang Prabang, neglected in the wake of the 1975 socialist revolution for its association with the royal family, eventually became a World Heritage Site and tourist attraction, a nostalgic space where French Indochina has somehow come to be glorified. During my fieldwork, while I was interviewing monks, tourists, heritage officials, and local inhabitants, I could not help but be drawn to anything that seemed to me particular and different. Specifically, I felt a great deal of empathy for the local residents of the town, troubled by now having to live in compliance with heritage regulations, unable to make modifications to their homes as they pleased. In contrast, I felt a great deal less empathy toward the UNESCO officials, who embodied for me European-style patrimonialist discourse; and even less so toward the tourists, who, despite mirroring my own nomadic inclinations, seemed to represent the bulldozer of globalization. And while I conducted interviews with as many categories of actor as I could find, my sympathies lay primarily with the local Lao, the indigenous population invaded by hordes of bourgeois tourists whose only motivation for preserving local customs was to consume them on vacation. Of course, I do not expect all anthropologists to identify with this somewhat acerbic description. Yet many among us are irresistibly drawn to the *indigenousness* of our interlocutors, whether close or far away. The anthropologist Dimitrios Theodossopoulos evoked his nostalgia as an ethnographer during his fieldwork among the Embera of Colombia quite superbly.[57] In an autobiographical tone, he shows how nostalgia for idealized traditional societies molded his first impressions as a researcher. As obvious as it may seem, anthropologists still need their "savages," their particular and different locals, who seem to contradict the idea of an undifferentiated modernity (which, as a matter of fact, they often want to embrace hungrily). To which I would add that participant observation functions precisely as a nostalgic search for intimacy and sincerity with locals. Most researchers aspire to relive the archetypal experience of the Malinowskian encounter, even with UNESCO experts or Wall Street traders.

Overall, though anthropologists today have turned their attention to people in power ("studying up"), in many cases their exonostalgia expresses itself through compassion for a fragile otherness. I agree with Zsuzsa Gille when she writes that, as anthropologists, "we only feel compassion towards the little people."[58] However, Henrika Kuklick argues that today, it is no longer the effects of colonial policies that are condemned by the discipline, but rather the "steamroller of globalization."[59] For example, in these times of never-ending crisis, the effects of globalization, the development of neoliberalism, and the increase in social insecurity, wars, and global warming are all new, often deadly threats for groups and individuals. Nowadays, the anthropologist's fragile other is less the endangered cultural savage, the powerless colonized figure (although this is still the case in certain regions of the world); no, today, it is more likely to be the poor, the weak, the suffering, the powerless facing social instability, urban poverty, economic migration, war, and political marginalization. Think only of Ruth Behar's *Translated Woman*, Patrick Declerck's *Les naufragés*, or Philippe Bourgois's *In Search of Respect*, those emblematic texts of contemporary anthropology, among many others besides. Like the first anthropologists, their tone too is pre-apocalyptic. "Too late" is their motto, while the specters of loss and crisis prevail. As for me, I am not surprised by the attachment anthropologists feel for the fragile, crisis-stricken little people. This attitude is profoundly rooted in their disciplinary exonostalgia, an indignation and a theoretical positioning in the face of irreversible loss. Above all, though, it reveals their commitment to the future. Nostalgia is intimately tied up with their desire to imagine a different world: one able to withstand cultural homogenization and preserve ethnic diversity, one where social and political recognition can be gained for all. Truly, even for anthropologists themselves, hope is never far from nostalgia.

4
The Plastic Anthropologist

In your role as anthropologists, to pretend you're being and doing
what you really are being and doing...a constant shifting of
identities, a blurring of positions and perspectives, you end up lost in a
kaleidoscope of masquerades, roles, general make-believe.
—Tom McCarthy, *Satin Island*

Observers of extinction and crisis, ever-nostalgic, anthropologists
are also, by the very nature of their work, able to shift between
different social and cultural horizons. "The victim of some kind
of chronic uprooting," writes Lévi-Strauss, "while traveling, the
ethnologist plays his position in the world, he crosses the limits."[1]
And yet anthropologists do not lose their culture, so to speak.
Instead, in conducting their research, especially through participant observation, they switch from one cultural or social repertoire
to the next, exploiting the human capacity for self-transformation,
this plasticity that *always already* characterizes us. The protagonist
in Woody Allen's comedy *Zelig* (1983), about a human chameleon
whose identity changes according to whom he is around (he
becomes fat among the obese, a Nazi among Nazis, black among
black people, etc.), offers a remarkable likeness to the contemporary
figure of the anthropologist. Not that anthropologists are always
human chameleons like Zelig; but in the repertoire of research
postures that they regularly deploy, there is an experiential pursuit

symbolic of our discipline (though something we share nowadays with comprehensive sociologists and qualitative specialists): and that is to try to live temporarily in the skin of others. I say "try," because this demands an effort of the imagination that can never quite be reached. To grasp others' intentions and emotions is an epistemic Grail, precisely because they are *theirs*, and I will never be this "other" whom I aim to approach and understand.[2] In this final chapter, based on a critical review of accounts of ethnographic experiences, I focus on the participatory side of anthropology and show to what extent this constitutes an existential and intellectual adventure involving complex human faculties, such as empathy, imitation, and "playing to be someone else." If we do not lose our culture, it is because anthropologists are marked by their ability to pass between cultures and contexts and to deploy multiple identifications.

Going Native

Let us start with a step back. The process of indigenizing an outsider is an operation that has existed as long as there have been intercultural exchanges. There are numerous examples of Westerners being captured by natives, only to become natives themselves. Consider Portuguese sailor Diogo Alvares Correia, also known as Caramuru, whose ship sank off the coast of Brazil in the fifteenth century. After being rescued by Tupinamba natives, he married the daughter of a chieftain and became a go-between for trade between Portuguese colonists and local populations. Yet such proximity also brings problems. During the colonial era, fear of cultural cross-contamination, rooted in the racism of the time, was such that an impermeable boundary had to be established between colonizers and colonized.[3] Fear of going native spread among colonists, who were discouraged from spending too much time with the locals or even dressing like them.[4] Frightening though they may be, distant colonized spaces also constituted, for some, heterotopias, liberated spaces—especially sexually—in comparison to the bourgeois values of Europe. Far away from it all, one may fall in love with much younger women (Gauguin) or men (Lawrence of Arabia), the kind of desire still fulfilled by today's sexual tourism (see chapter 2). And the trope of Westerners being *too* immersed in local mores still pervades contemporary popular culture (in films such as *Dances with Wolves* or James Cameron's *Avatar*).

At the end of the nineteenth century, participation became a central precept of a scientific project to describe otherness. No need to revisit the methodological foundations systematized by Malinowksi (encouraging scholars to leave behind the colonial missions and offices and venture out among the indigenous populations). From then on, seeking to understand the native perspective from the inside in the pursuit of scientific knowledge became the cornerstone of our discipline. There were, of course, many who continued their research à la Griaule, bringing their informants to their tent or veranda. Malinowski himself was not such a fervent participant, as we can see from his *Diary*.[5] Yet many of his successors put the master's advice into practice. During her fieldwork among the Lesu of Papua in 1930, Hortense Powdermaker took part in a rite in front of 2,000 people: "The drums began; I danced. Something happened. I forgot myself and was one with the dancers. Under the full moon and for the brief time of the dance, I ceased to be an anthropologist from a modern society. I danced. When it was over I realized that, for this short period, I had been emotionally part of the rite."[6] Later, when describing her participant experience among African Americans in the Mississippi town of Indianola, Powdermaker expresses how much she "enjoyed the participation. I am the kind of person who likes to participate";[7] however, she always "remained an anthropologist."[8] Indeed, it was the absence of participation and strong emotional investment that made her research among Hollywood producers so boring; she never "felt its culture in my bones"[9] the way she had among the Lesu and residents of Indianola.

During his various stints of fieldwork in Africa, Evans-Pritchard professed to have had "a hut and byre like theirs; I went hunting with them with spear and bow and arrow; I learned to make pots; I consulted oracles; and so forth,"[10] all to "understand how and why Africans are doing certain things."[11] Similarly, Michel Leiris participated actively in religious ceremonies, to the extent that Griaule would occasionally reproach him for his excessive proximity to local customs. In *Phantom Africa*, one senses how torn Leiris is between the contemporary imperatives of his discipline, "the inhuman position of being an observer,"[12] and his desire to take part, a desire he would eventually give in to, "possessed"[13] among the possessed women of Gondar in Ethiopia. "I can no longer bear methodical research," he wrote. "I need to immerse myself in their drama, to touch their ways of being, to soak in the live flesh."[14] There are countless other examples of anthropologists who, before the 1970s, helped consolidate participation as an experience and research method, though written traces are often harder to find, limited to introductory passages or unpublished field notes. Interestingly, as demonstrated by Powdermaker or Leiris, it is the emotional side of anthropological participation that prevails, going on to become a central theme from the 1970s on.

With the experiential shift of the 1970s and '80s, participation definitely lost all negative connotations. Following on from the seminal texts of Favret-Saada on the French side,[15] and the success of North American postmodernism,[16] the participant experience of anthropology, the intimacy nurtured with one's interlocutors, one's "friends" (a revealing term) on the ground, became highly prized. Loïc Wacquant argues that one should "'go native' but 'go native armed,' that is, equipped with your theoretical and methodological tools. . . . Go ahead, go native, but come back a sociologist."[17] In fact, the position of anthropologists remains *always already* "in-between,"[18] torn between the academic world and the one they seek to take part in. Though there are those too who cross over and never come back, like Colin Turnbull, who settled in India to be ordained as a Buddhist monk by the Dalai Lama. Like Conrad's Kurtz, these examples serve as a line not to be crossed for a discipline that has now become fully participatory, but does not want to become completely subjectivist, even solipsist, either. Without quite going native, we may at least aspire to become "bicultural."[19]

The public image of the heroic anthropologist of the Malinowskian era is now mirrored by that of the "pathetic anthropologist":[20] a vulnerable scholar whose invocation of the pathetic, the visceral, and the physical brings an epistemological touch of soul to research. Often, the topic under investigation is presented as requiring anthropologists to engage in worlds whose emotional intensity proves particularly powerful. The field of religious anthropology, for instance, historically dominated by militant atheists (with the notable exceptions of Evans-Pritchard and Victor Turner), teems with examples of taking part in ritual practices or reflections on the question itself of taking part: must one be initiated in order to describe the process of initiation?[21]

Sometimes, anthropologists' accounts of their participatory experiences depict them in violent situations that constitute a threat to both their physical and moral integrity. Between 1982 and 1984, Patrick Declerck would occasionally, one night, put himself "in the skin of a homeless man" to "try to feel in my bones what they feel";[22] much like Philippe Bourgois, who provides a detailed account of his dangerous life among the crack dealers of El Barrio in New York;[23] and Loïc Wacquant, leading "a sort of Jekyll-and-Hyde existence,"[24] who spent his day boxing and his nights "writing social theory,"[25] switching between his "gut" and his "intellect."[26] When for four months in the 1980s, Anne Allison tried to step into the shoes of a club hostess in Tokyo, this often unpleasant experience forced her to "accept the subordinate and sometimes servile position of servicer" in a phallocratic world (particularly the constant remarks about her differing physique, and the need to continually flatter even insulting men).[27] However, for the most part, participation is presented as a paramount requirement in the pursuit of knowledge. Without it, there would be no way of understanding the impulses behind witchcraft in France, or what drives boxing culture in American ghettos. Ultimately, this requirement is imposed by the "field" itself, which is too complex, too opaque, and too emotional to be fully grasped from a bird's-eye view; the participatory call of the wild seems too strong to resist.

Empathy

My working hypothesis is as follows: acting the human chameleon is one the central points of attraction, both existential and intellectual, in participant research. I now examine the foundations of such a plastic disposition, the cognitive and emotional competences it requires, although each anthropologist engages these differently. Participation is, more than anything, an empathic experience intended to gather information on others. It results in the acquisition of this precious, tacit knowledge possessed by the actors involved, and which goes unspoken. As an emotional act, it consists in the anthropologist trying to experience the same emotions felt by his or her interlocutors, which may happen involuntarily. In fact, our emotions can sometimes align with those of our subjects. During the breakup of his famous cockfight, for example, Clifford Geertz and his wife took to their heels and fled like everyone else, a quasi-instinctive reaction that, in the spirit of urgency, earned them the trust of their Balinese interlocutors.[28] And while Philippe Bourgois was hanging out in Harlem with the crack smokers and dealers for three years, he spent one night buying drugs with his informants, going with them to their dens to watch them shoot up, filled with dread and adrenaline, but also becoming attuned to what it was like to fear the cops and buy drugs on the street.[29] Most of the time, the anthropologist's interpretative performance consists in striving to *think* as someone else. This ability to understand internally is as imaginative as it is emotional, blending the exercise of imagination with a "transmutation of sensibilities."[30] Thomas Csordas describes three religious participant experiences (a divine prophecy in the company of evangelists; a vision among the Navajo; and a mystical experience after taking peyote) during which he underwent such a transmutation of sensibilities that, with considerable cognitive effort, they allowed him to imagine the nature of these phenomena, without being converted or going native. On reflection, it is these imaginative and emotional peaks that characterize the experience of anthropological participation. Combining emotional empathy with cognitive inferences, these exercises are generally effectuated within the framework of a voluntary and conscious mechanism deployed by the researcher, albeit sometimes involuntarily and with unexpected results, such as Geertz's great escape. There are many anthropologists who have described, for example, how, after months of research, they found themselves using witchcraft-based language to explain an affliction.[31]

As we now know, empathy is not an exclusively human faculty. Some primates are also able to understand what is going on in the heads of other members of their species; it has even been theorized that great apes possess a "theory of mind."[32] But only humans appear to have the special capacity to put themselves in others' places, which allows them to grasp "more completely than any other animal what others feel and what they might need."[33] What anthropologists are doing during their participant experience is pushing this human capacity to its limits. Of course, the history of anthropology has demonstrated that empathic identification does not work in the same way for all categories of actor, and anthropologists also have their favorites, those historically constituted alterities that merit the effort required for empathy. But it is also a question of the foundations of human (and animal) altruism. In addition to being professional intruders and foreigners, anthropologists are also professional empathizers (even when this can at times turn to antipathy, itself a potential gateway to knowledge).[34]

Imitation

While participation engages emotional and imaginative mechanisms relating to empathy, it also involves a competence in imitation. It is a truism that to put oneself in another's shoes, one must go through different stages of imitation; anthropologists, before they can master them naturally, try to "replicate the gestures, words, appearances and actions of other individuals they take as models."[35] In his *Poetics*, Aristotle wrote how inclined humans were toward imitation, acquiring their first knowledge by it, and taking pleasure from it. The latter alludes to the pleasure felt in the contemplation of art imitating reality, of theatrical make-believe. But anthropologists in the field are not artists: what they do is not performance, and the concept of imitation must be employed here in its broadest sense. For humans, imitation acquires a unique dimension insofar as it not only allows us to replicate, but is also rooted in a capacity to identify the intentions of another active subject that can be imitated. What distinguishes humans from other species in particular is that they understand mental states *recursively*, that is, intentions and beliefs are represented that "have a bearing on other mental states (other intentions, other beliefs)."[36] They are able to meta-represent and imitate quite accurately. The empathy we feel for people, together with what psychologists call "ostensive communication," can facilitate these imitation mechanisms.

For participant anthropologists, the faculty of imitation is often enacted intentionally within the context of understanding new cultural and linguistic repertoires: "doing as others do," which, especially during the first moments in the field, makes it possible for researchers to assimilate some of what their interlocutors say and do, resulting in the acquisition of new postures, accents, and habits. As the only white person in a line of people buying crack in New York, on one occasion Bourgois imitated his informants and joined in the chorus of recrimination aimed at one customer who was buying too much, instantly feeling a sense of "comfort and security."[37] Within the framework of his research among the homeless of Paris, Declerck decided to let himself be "rounded up incognito by the police along with the others."[38] The hellish days and nights spent as one of the down and outs consisted in doing as others do: sleeping rough, passively begging, being arrested. For him, the upheaval of this temporary homelessness constituted a veritable exercise in camouflage, clothed as he was "in an old pair of pants tied with a string instead of a belt, two stained T-shirts, a torn leather jacket, and ripped shoes. A paint-splattered hat and a scarf helped me disguise my face, which otherwise might have been recognized."[39]

Declerck's undercover experience represents an extreme situation that many anthropologists will not identify with. Generally speaking, imitation is a voluntary technique that allows the human chameleon to constantly refine his attempt at integration and gradually be forgotten about by his interlocutors. In Wacquant's case, it took months of practicing together with other boxers, spending his days at the gym and "gloving-up" for them to finally share with him "their joys and sorrows, their dreams and their setbacks, their picnics, evenings out dancing, and family excursions,"[40] and invite him to take part in their politico-religious meetings, "the only European non-believer among ten thousand entranced African-American faithful."[41] Even in the 1930s, during her audacious research among African American communities in Mississippi, Hortense Powdermaker remarked how, without going so far as to imitate the dress or appearance of her subjects, she started to take on the "color" of her field of study. As a result of her time in local restaurants, hotels, and churches, she was often perceived as a woman of color by her white interlocutors, while "a rumor spread among them that I was really Negro. . . . I suppose this was the only way they could account for me, since I differed so much from every other white person with whom they had any contact."[42] In the segregated world of 1930s America, the participation of Malinowski's student, this white Jewish American woman, in African American life is an exemplary case of the woman chameleon. Although we know that this kind of discourse also forms part of a romantic rhetoric relating to integration invoked by generations of anthropologists, there is a type of mimicry involved in the participatory effort: the attempt to blend into a new environment and get into the skin of one's interlocutors, by adopting mimetic behaviors, often voluntarily.[43]

Playing to Be Someone Else

Now we must go even further in our analysis. For anthropological mimicry is also a question of acting. In many ethnographic experiences, "doing as" actually becomes "doing as *if one is*," where the "as if" introduces the idea of a role to play, and the distance the role affords us as anthropologists in the lives of our interlocutors during participation. Powdermaker's, Wacquant's, Bourgois's, and Declerck's accounts of their ethnographic experiences evoke Sartre's description in *Being and Nothingness* of a waiter in a café "playing at being a waiter in a café": having adopted the costume, the attitude and the language,

> his movement is quick and forward, a little too precise, a little too rapid. He comes toward the patrons with a step a little too quick. He bends forward a little too eagerly; his voice, his eyes express an interest a little too solicitous for the order of the customer. Finally, there he returns, trying to imitate in his walk the inflexible stiffness of some kind of automaton while carrying his tray with the recklessness of a tight-rope-walker. . . . All his behavior seems to us a game. . . . He is playing, he is amusing himself. But what is he playing? We need not watch long before we can explain it: he is playing at being a waiter in a café.[44]

Many important questions arise from this text. First of all, the young man's mimicry, crude and exaggerated, that of someone who takes his role seriously. We must also acknowledge the pleasure felt by the actor. In a great many circumstances, while engaged in scientific exercise to gather data that would otherwise remain inaccessible, participating anthropologists are also playing at being homeless among the homeless, a Pentecostalist among Pentecostalists, or even a boxer among boxers. They are playing at being another. To this end, anthropologists will sometimes put on makeup, dress up, and engage in a performance, one that may have a theatrical, reflexive, conscious, and voluntary aspect, especially during the first days in the field. But, as Sartre continues, "The game is a kind of marking out and investigation. The child plays with his body in order to explore it, to take inventory of it; the waiter in the café plays with his condition in order to realize it."[45]

This is a crucial point, insofar as it touches on the very nature of ethnographic learning (and learning in general). Indeed, it is in playing a role, which can be a source of pleasure and suffering, that researchers are able to deploy their emotional empathy and imagination. On the subject of Zande oracles, Evans-Pritchard remarked that he had to "act as though [he] trusted the Zande oracles . . . whatever reservations I might have."[46] By doing as if, he added, "one ends in believing or half-believing, as one acts."[47] Much like Quesalid, Lévi-Strauss's skeptic-turned-shaman (from his *Structural Anthropology*), Evans-Pritchard gradually came to accept Zande notions of witchcraft: "I had no choice," he writes.[48] This is somewhat reminiscent of Agnes, a young transgender American woman, whose transition Garfinkel observed and analyzed. To learn how to act like a woman, Agnes often "did as if," through daily interactions incognito that allowed her to grasp the rules "of conduct, appearance, skills, feelings, motives, and aspirations" of a real woman.[49] In contrast to Agnes's clandestine approach depicted by Garfinkel, participating anthropologists often learn openly in front of their interlocutors, but like Agnes, their "doing as if" is similarly rooted in the "continuous project of self-improvement" of their performance.[50]

Absorbed for a time by their role, generally transformed, enriched, even damaged by it, anthropologists are well aware that the experience of playing at being another is temporary, though it may be repeated on another occasion. This undoubtedly makes it even more exhilarating, or, in some cases, bearable. As Declerck wrote, "It is absolutely abysmal, terrifying, but at the same time, the reality is much worse than anything I experienced, because, for me, as soon as I am done, or sick of it, I can go home, take a shower, and move onto other things, unlike the homeless, who are in it for life."[51] For all that participating anthropologists become masters in the art of passing (Garfinkel's term), doing as if in order to learn and accumulate ethnographic data, it is also a chance for them to leave themselves, a heterotopic quality that I will explore in the following pages.

To understand the desire to participate and the pleasure that can come of it, we must further develop this third dimension, closely related to the desire to empathize and imitate: participation as leaving the self. There is something fundamentally heterotopic about participation in the field, a contextual operation that enables anthropologists to play around with the very foundations of their social identities, "the established 'me' of one's self-affirmation."[52] Evans-Pritchard aptly remarked how an anthropologist becomes "at least temporarily a sort of double marginal man, alienated from both worlds."[53] In the same vein, Powdermaker described how much her different experiences of research allowed her to step "beyond the boundaries of [her] background,"[54] seeing the exercise of anthropology as "continuously stepping in and out of their society."[55] Is *Phantom Africa* not Leiris's account of the African itinerary of a man on the lookout for a new skin to live in, though he admits by the end of his adventure to "remain[ing] the same man, riddled with anxiety, . . . a kind of 'bourgeois' artist"?[56]

Not only—and this is a truism—does this stepping in and out of ourselves weaken the solid core of certain parts of our identity; we are also engaging in a veritable exercise in "disidentity."[57] This is not a question of "renouncing one's identity,"[58] or of no longer having one at all (there are always new identities to be ascribed in the field); yet in participant observation, there are certain aspects of our established "me," sometimes the most intimate ones, that may, for a time only, be set aside. Remember Powdermaker's claims that, in the short space of a Lesu dance, she "ceased to be an anthropologist from a modern society";[59] or in Indianola, she sometimes found herself wondering "whether [she] was Negro or white."[60] Indeed, from academia to the field, the anthropologist's self can be quite unstable. As an example, let us consider our sense of morality as discussed by the late Ruwen Ogien in one of his latest books. Some tests in experimental philosophy have proven that the existence of stable moral personality types is debatable, and that "personalities do not have a 'hard core' that is consistent and uniform, unchanging from one situation to another."[61] As Ogien sets out, any factor may direct our behavior toward the moral or immoral, such as the simple smell of hot croissants wafting across a supermarket, which has been shown to increase the likelihood of individuals taking pity on beggars and giving them money. It is not hard to imagine that, in the emotionally complex and loaded situations that arise from ethnographic fieldwork, an anthropologist's moral compass may be marked by relative instability. Lévi-Strauss himself outlined this variability in his affirmation that anthropologists, often left-wing progressives at home, are quick to become right-wing conservatives abroad in their efforts to preserve traditions. Consider too the borderline experience of Kenneth Good, whose participation in the lives of the Yanomami proved intense and controversial, to the point that he married a fifteen-year-old girl, Yarima (whom he met when she was nine).[62] In the context of their lives, this kind of behavior, morally unacceptable in the United States, for the Yanomami was not only moral but in fact desirable (as Good puts it, to facilitate his integration). Similarly, in his time among the crack dealers in Harlem, Philippe Bourgois took part in and supported certain practices that he would consider morally reprehensible within the context of his normal life. Of course, today, more so than before, anthropologists are encouraged to operate according to the same code of ethics in the field as they would at home. However, many researchers would argue that such moral deviations are part and parcel of an anthropologist's effort to integrate, or may even be preexisting, though I find it very difficult to distinguish between the personal, moral, and professional stakes involved. Suffice it to say that the human chameleon's participant experience often entails a moral adjustment, for better or worse.

Generally speaking, participatory fieldwork makes it possible, in the space of a few months or years, to *imagine* oneself, in certain aspects, to be a Jew among Jews, gay among gays, African among Africans, poor among the poor, and so on. Through this kind of disassociation, "relieved at no longer being shackled to oneself,"[63] the anthropologist's "I" glimpses the possibility of becoming "another," of surpassing the limits of self-identification, and embodying, temporarily and fragmentarily, Rimbaud's "I is another." There is almost certainly something intoxicating in this displacement of identity, a certain hubris, the founding principles of which can be compared to other figures of disidentity. I am thinking, for example, of those practices that rest on the register of the destabilizing shift between identity and otherness: acting, writing, cosplaying, possession (where the self becomes another, possessed by an invisible entity that speaks through it), cannibalism (which involves absorbing another's identity to become stronger), or the drag queen's performance (where the self can be transformed into someone else to denounce, with gusto, the gendered world it inhabits).

As I have mentioned, participation constitutes an often temporary exercise in disidentity. There are many participant anthropologists who recount how, though tempted to go native, they were still able to revert quickly to their academic habitus (like Wacquant, who even considered putting his university career on hold to become a professional boxer). And yet the experience of playing at being another has rarely allowed those who undertake it to escape unscathed, though most believe that these aftereffects should be kept private. It left Leiris with a sense of melancholy, finally realizing that "the journey only changes us occasionally. Most of the time you remain sadly as you ever were,"[64] a bleak acknowledgment that the "I," though transformed, does not become another. As Devereux demonstrated, the experience of participation also provokes a number of anxieties, in particular due to the "partition between subject and observer."[65] For example, "anxieties may arise when an ethnologist finds himself attracted to the lifestyle of a tribe whose behavior would be taboo in his own society,"[66] an attitude embodied by Kenneth Good's experience among the Yanomami. Often, one's professional position and the rhetoric of cultural relativism can lessen the anxiety linked to the destabilizing process of leaving certain aspects of the self behind, those defense mechanisms that allow us to "carefully sterilize the affect."[67] But does this academic and literary distancing not simultaneously dull the pleasure born of having taken part, or even communed with others during these privileged moments?

Overall, the experience of participation, transgressive and transformational as it is, is described as glorious, similar to a rite of passage. For many, it actually proves to be stabilizing, not only as a professionally recognized scientific method within the discipline, but as a vehicle for a repertoire of multicultural and relativist values that these days are highly prized among Western elites. To make a light comparison with the figure of a cannibal, anthropologists who participate are playing at being another in order to become even more themselves, and stabilize certain aspects of their social identity at home, be it professional or personal. Above all, it should be noted that there are many different ways of implementing these empathic and imitative faculties. Distributed unequally among ethnologists, some use and master these better than others; there are even those who succeed, more easily than others, in taking part in multiple different cultural environments, becoming pluricultural or capable of maintaining a principle of detachment across multiple worlds. In these cases, it is as if "doing as if" becomes a second skin. Gradually, a stabilized heterotopia emerges from the foundations of one's turbulent beginnings, the result of having become a human chameleon, a specialist of temporary disidentity.

Conclusion

For a Cultural and Patrimonial Diplomacy

> An interest in genealogy took hold of people.... From all sides the
> need to know one's roots grew. Identity...was becoming a major
> concern.... It was something that people had to possess, rediscover,
> conquer, assert, express. A precious and supreme asset.
> —Annie Ernaux, *Les années*

I would like to end this short book by addressing a series of theoretical and ethical questions on the desire to transmit culture and
contemporary patrimonial nostalgia, questions that anthropology
allows us to consider in depth. Nowadays, all over the globe,
culture and heritage (as well as identity and roots) represent an
often-indisputable collective self-affirmation within a context of
globalization and detachment from one's roots. The preservation
and defense of one's culture, as well as the rediscovery of one's roots,
are now considered fundamental, inalienable rights. But there is
more to it than that. In Western societies, positively speaking,
identity policies do provide a register for a right to difference, the
other side of the coin sadly being the risk of ghettoization. Coun-
tering the essentialism of Enlightenment universalism can often
lead to replacing it with other equally essentialist perspectives.
Ethnic and cultural absolutism, strongly condemned by Paul Gilroy,[1] is never far away, as some consider it their political mission to

destroy imitation seen as a loss of *one's* own culture, a parody of real, authentic culture. At the hour of the so-called clash of civilizations, the debate surrounding difference can be a minefield; proceed with caution.

In truth, the issue of the right to discuss the identity and culture of *others* is the main point of friction. You may well understand, but only I can say it. Not unlike how Jacques Derrida says, "In a certain way . . . 'I am the last of the Jews,' 'I am the end of Judaism,' that is the death of Judaism, but also its only chance to survive, I am the last to be able to say this, no one else has the right."[2] Speaking for someone else, especially about a history and culture of oppression and trauma, is often understood as "Is he with us or against us?"[3]

At the same time, anthropologists are increasingly concerned to see social actors invoking these culturalist categories in such absolutist terms, even if they themselves continue to use them, albeit cautiously.[4] Of course, humans, for all their biological unity, are distinguished by their cultural diversity, so we need a fitting concept able to describe the diversity of languages and histories pertaining to these different human groups. But in this era of globalization and transnational movements, it is problematic to speak of cultures, in the sense of clearly outlined entities with well-defined contours, attached to a specific territory and language. This is the age of the movement of individuals, objects, and ideas; of forming ever larger collectives; of blending populations; and of neverending exchanges; all of which this thin notion of culture hardly suffices to describe. If the sense of having an autobiographical self constitutes a universal psychological given (and the narrative that goes with it), it is infinitely more complicated to determine just how many cultures (two, three, ten?) we stand to inherit. We must follow the strands of complex narrative identities, the meanderings of which comprise multiple different figures of otherness that intercross and intermingle, where all sorts of contradictions, hesitations, and uncertainties are found.[5] One is many. "I" is others.

In short, there is a risk of turning categories of culture and identity into caricatures, which often only serves to reinforce the lines between social and cultural realities that are in fact much more complex. Introducing differences and putting up cultural walls can prove a highly dangerous undertaking, especially in politics. As early as 1930, Freud wrote in *Civilization and Its Discontents* that we should endeavor to guard "against the enthusiastic prejudice which holds that our civilization is the most precious thing that we possess or could acquire."[6] The rhetoric of culture, beyond the openness and diversity the term implies, also has a dark side. Behind the necessary recognition of cultural diversity and the wealth it brings, there also lurk powerful mechanisms of exclusion and self-isolation.

When threatened, faced with the permanent risk of loss, culture becomes an even more precious commodity. Nowadays, the notion of endangered cultures is tied up in a host of interconnecting personal, scientific, and political agendas, from the most beneficial to the most pernicious. It is easy to understand the personal or collective curiosity to know where we come from and to remember nostalgically; we want to share that desire to transmit culture held by populations historically forced to forget or abandon their cultural practices. The duty to remember, intolerable when invoked to serve a nationalist device that prescribes "the" good and unique memory,[7] represents a legitimate call to action for millions of individuals who want to see their trauma acknowledged. We often forget that memory policies relating to the Holocaust constitute a beneficial "referential framework."[8] To name just one example, playing Claude Lanzmann's documentary *Shoah* in Nanjing in 2004 (where 300,000 Chinese were massacred by Japanese soldiers in 1937) for a Chinese audience was the key to unlocking a discourse on suffering and trauma.[9] As post-Holocaust memories were reawakened, the subsequent establishment of international criminal tribunals, and in particular "truth and reconciliation" commissions (as in South Africa, Rwanda, Argentina, and so on) saw the question of trauma finally being taken seriously,[10] though often at great cost.[11] Now more than ever, a politics of care must be pursued for today's and yesterday's victims, those who have been discriminated against, colonized, or exterminated. In a democratic society, the duty of memory does not belong to particular groups; any group of victims is free to use it reflexively, and to attempt to carve out a memory space for its own history. I am not demanding the "sacralization of memory,"[12] that is, that it should be impervious to criticism and debate, but rather that the domain of memory should be extended under the watchful gaze of professional historians (who are, ultimately, the defenders of history), while seeking what Paul Ricoeur called for: "une mémoire juste."[13]

On the other hand, it is problematic to witness the rhetoric of cultural loss being used in absolutist terms. Today's imperative to transmit tends to obscure any need to forget. These days, are we even able to forget, to throw away and destroy? In his short story "Funes, His Memory," Jorge Luis Borges presents a man who, after falling from his horse, is no longer able to forget, a form of hypermnesia that leads him straight to death's door. In fact, forgetting is a vital process. People, groups, monuments, and practices have (unfortunately) always been made to disappear. Loss is a given of existence. As painful as it is, cultivating an "art of losing," as Elizabeth Bishop's superb poem reminds us,[14] seems to be one of the conditions of our lives. And some prefer not to remember, not to transmit, to be allowed not to go on. Without falling into praise of oblivion, as David Rieff does,[15] it is particularly concerning to see this rhetoric being used to nationalist, paternalist, and racist ends aiming to set in stone the "right" culture that should be transmitted. It is worrying to see it twisted by "roots" cults, simplistic and false identitarian discourses that promote transparency of origins. My anthropologist's quarrel with the—often intransigent—defenders of precious culture comes primarily from the way they underestimate, even ignore, the creative capacity of humans to reinvent, going forward, new aesthetic, social, and cultural forms. My incompatibility with their moral, often declinist, position stems from the fact that, for fifty years now, anthropologists, who have themselves historically been mired in exonostalgia, continue to demonstrate the vitality of human cultures, all of which are endowed with capacities for innovation and sophistication that change with time, based on processes of borrowing and exchanging. In the end, this constitutes *the* main dilemma when it comes to heritage: how to maintain historical ties to the past without falling into conservatism. While this book is certainly not claiming for a tabula rasa, I hope it succeeded at triggering more reflexivity about heritage practices.

With demand for cultural preservation growing around the world, the aim of this book has been, predominantly, to demonstrate the multiple forms that diagnoses of cultural loss take. The ethnographic data that I gathered over the past years, in Guinea-Conakry, in Laos, and in UNESCO offices around the globe, call into question concepts of loss, permanence, memory, transmission, and heritage in these societies. In so doing, they invite us to reflect in turn on our relationship with heritage and memory, both our own and those of others. First of all, I believe it is crucial to understand how and why certain individuals develop a unique, personal attachment to heritage. Walter Benjamin already posited the dilemma of patrimonial identification when he said, *"For what is the value of all our culture if it is divorced from experience?"*[16] One of the major challenges UNESCO faces is to create a common heritage in the absence of any identification with its policies. As I have shown, there are many people involved in the heritage process, from those who are passionately committed to preservation to those who are indifferent. Many of us have met these heritage militants in the field, whose desire for preservation always seems defined as a lonely struggle against the "bad" locals, the "wrong" materials, the "corrupt" local authorities, and the "ignorant" tourists. I have demonstrated that nostalgia is an important driving force for such heritage makers, a yearning for historical grandeur that materializes through architectural and cultural reproductions from the past, often combining a strong emotional attachment to places or objects with an articulate scholarly discourse on the arts and culture of the region. But in between these extremes lies a continuum of individuals with diverse interests and motivations with regard to heritage; many examples of people living in poverty who turn to heritage primarily for financial reasons; or expatriates who become the main representatives of tradition in town. Why do some individuals build an intimate relationship with an object or a place to the extent that they become conservation developers or amateur preservationists? Can anybody become a heritagizer? Why do some people turn into heritage militants, identify with heritage, feel deeply about it, value it, and then decide to actively protect it, the way others develop a passion for nature and the protection of the environment?[17] What constitutes the base ingredients of the heritage desire? In this book, I have shown that the desire for heritage rests on the assumption that a place, an object, or a cultural practice, objectified as *unique*, is *threatened*. And that it also presupposes some anxiety about *irreversibility*, a feeling about the passing of time seen as irreversible (heritage being the human antidote to this temporal inevitability). Family, peers, school education, and the media play an absolutely fundamental role, as they constitute the social scaffolding through which attention to heritage is created and reinforced. More importantly, ideas of threat and irreversibility must be inserted into a personal narrative. To me, this is one of the crucial aspects to comprehending heritage desire. Heritage defenders always have a story of themselves to tell about the *relation* they have with the place, the object, or the practice. This narrative is biographical. Usually highly emotional, it deploys the relational epistemology that was woven between a nostalgic individual and the heritage to be preserved. Through the narrative, loss is mine. And even if it was not my loss, it *becomes* mine.

Next, anthropologists observe the universalization of a specific type of rhetoric and heritage practices, those dictated by UNESCO in particular. The diagnoses of loss and the remedies proposed by the institution have an international aura, and are now globalized tools. Roland Robertson rightly speaks of the globalization of "the nostalgic attitude."[18] From a collective point of view, heritage, particularly as defined by UNESCO, has become a central issue, not only for governments and groups of individuals, but also for public opinion around the world, often highly emotive. It can become the epicenter for political tensions, national and international, as with the Buddhas of Bamiyan in 2001. It is hard to forget the images of these giant statues being dynamited and destroyed by the Afghan Taliban, a testament to the country's pre-Islamic past, but also to the international community's inability to prevent such acts. More recently, the mausoleums of Timbuctoo, ancient places of prayer for many inhabitants of the city and the wider region, were demolished by Islamist zealots. Some governments, in turn, try to use the heritage label to nationalist ends, meaning that a site's designation by UNESCO can lead to serious international tensions and identitarian passions. There is, for instance, the abiding memory of the armed tensions between Cambodia and Thailand surrounding the Khmer temple of Preah Vihear, which was listed by UNESCO in 2008 as a Cambodian site, something long pursued by the Thai authorities.[19] Though it seeks to be a peacemaking organization dedicated to human cross-cultural understanding, UNESCO and its heritage label have instead occasionally promoted chauvinism and nationalist pride. Insofar as it mobilizes the trope of endangered culture, patrimonialist rhetoric runs the risk in particular of reinforcing one desire: to be bound to oneself; to be curled in on one's own cultural condition. Jean-Pierre Warnier's observation is more apt now than ever: "The biggest danger facing humanity's cultural future is neither the disappearance of tradition from culture . . . nor the uniformization of cultures in the world, nor the Americanization of peoples, but rather the Balkanization of cultural references and the absence of a universal narrative setting out the future of the diversity and cultural unity of the human race."[20]

So then, what to do? The human chameleon, this plastic role that anthropologists assume in their fieldwork—does this constitute a future for humanity? Should we support this politics of undecidability that constructivists such as Judith Butler[21] and Donna Haraway[22] urge us to pursue? Yes, we should certainly seek to destabilize categories of culture, identities, and roots by demonstrating how unstable they are, mobilized through specific historical and cultural regimes of power. Along the way, we can indulge in an inventory of our visceral attachments, to be the Spinoza of our belongings. Anthropology as a technique of participation, imitation, and leaving the self also has a fine lesson to teach us. For, if social and cultural contrasts truly do exist, human beings are in possession of universal reflexive capacities that allow them to switch identities and to imaginatively put themselves in someone else's place. From a cognitive perspective, we all share the same disposition toward meta-representation, toward imagination. I understand the concern, fear even, that some have in seeing the complexity of their reality described by someone that they consider an outsider to their experience. But is there not in all of us a certain amount of suffering and otherness that allows us to imagine the experience and oppression of another? More so than other species, humans have that special capacity to empathize, to feel, often concurrently, the pleasure and pain of others. Whether we want to or not is another matter . . .

Like Sisyphus, anthropologists have their own rock to push. Eternally nostalgic and self-reflexive, they treat their own identity problems by imagining themselves in others' shoes, and so better understand them. These are their ethics. But they also believe in the possibility of establishing constructive dialogues. In his latest book, *Enquête sur les modes d'existence*, Bruno Latour[23] describes the work of a diplomat as successfully finding the right word to talk about and with someone else.[24] Finding the right word, being able to describe another's reality without causing offense by the violence of the language used, for them to remain open to dialogue, constitutes an extremely complex exercise. For there are words that function as weapons, those that have such a profound, magical, performative effect, that, uttered in a highly emotive context, preclude any basis of exchange. In these tense times of rising nationalism and populism, against the maelstrom of violent words, essentializations, caricatures, and "Are you with us or against us?," what we need are more Latourian diplomats, those individuals capable of interpreting and contributing to the debate, a laborious undertaking to be sure, but vital nonetheless.

Acknowledgments

This book is the result of long years of intellectual joy, painstaking work, collegial knowledge-sharing, and numerous anxieties. So many people have helped in bringing it to term, either through their active support, their criticism (well-meaning or otherwise!), their proofreading of different versions of the text, or just by being there. My heartfelt thanks to the following: Maria Sigutina, Olivia Angé, Charles Piot, Holly High, Bill Bissell, Laurent Legrain, Christoph Brumann, Michael Herzfeld, Edgar Tasia, Mathieu Hilgers, Gina Aït-Medhi, David Parkin, Bruno Latour, Adeline Masquelier, Thibault De Meyer, Thomas Ericksen, Maurice Bloch, Peter Geschiere, Philippe Jespers, Ruwen Ogien, David Eubelen, Michael Houseman, Rick Schweder, Pierre Petit, Mikaela Le Meur, Ruy Blanes, Laurent Berger, Joel Noret, Thomas Gennen, Filip De Boeck, Ramon Sarró, Anya Bernstein, Olivier Morin, Joseph Levy, Arnaud Halloy, the Dandy Warhols, Ulf Hannerz, Daniel Fabre, Philippe Descola, Yves Winkin, Jennifer Cole, Arjun Appadurai, Christine Langlois, Michael Lambek, Katharina Niemeyer, Vlad Naumescu, Mike Rowlands, Damiana Otoiu, Birgit Meyer, Pierre Guédant, Tara Gujadhur, Olivier Evrard, Nicolas Adell, Vinciane Desprets, Gil Bartholeyns, Nathalie Heinich, Gérard Lenclud, Anne Allison, Michael Stewart, Jean-Pierre Jacques, Manon Istasse, Alexandre Laumonnier, Kimberly Guinta, Chiara Bortolotto, Olivier Allard, Lynn Meskell, Janine Hamel, Charles Berliner, Muriel Berliner, Hervé Camara, Mama Salé Camara, Karifa Traoré, Télivel Diallo, Abou Soumah, Manivanh Thoummabout, Vileut Chitdara, Aaron Ponce, and the National Fund for Scientific Research (FNRS). A special thanks to the generations of students who contributed to enrich my thinking on these issues. All of the above, and many others besides (whose omission I can only apologize for), have helped me in developing this book's ideas—but I alone must bear the final responsibility for them.

This book comprises articles that have appeared in various scientific publications over the past few years. They have been extensively rewritten, brought up to date, and finalized to ensure a coherent and original commentary. The introduction expands on ideas from Berliner 2013d. Chapter 1 reworks ideas from Berliner 2005b, 2005c, 2007, and 2009; chapter 2 develops on Berliner 2010b, 2012, and 2013c; chapter 3 is an amended version of Berliner 2014a and 2014b; and chapter 4 reproduces reflections originally published in Berliner 2013c. I appreciate the permissions given to reuse this work in its new form.

Notes

Introduction

1. Jankélévitch 1974: 299. For detailed case studies and a theoretical comparison, I refer the reader to an edited volume by Olivia Ange and myself (2014).
2. A term coined by Robert Musil in *The Man without Qualities* (2004) to denote the acceleration of modern temporality.
3. Regarding the history of nostalgia, see Jankélévitch 1974 and Starobinski 1966.
4. Cassin 2013.
5. For a fascinating example of such commercialized nostalgia, see Ange research about Le Pain Quotidien (2015).
6. Herzfeld 2007: 175.
7. Ibid.
8. Rosaldo 1989: 107.
9. Appadurai 1996: 78.
10. Baudelaire 1869: 49.
11. Davis (1979) is the most comprehensive sociological account of the deployment of a nostalgic culture in the United States from the '70s.
12. See an excellent piece by Bartholeyns (2014) on this subject.
13. Reynolds 2012: ix.
14. For an analysis of contemporary nostalgic consumption in the United States, see Gary Cross (2015).
15. See Serres 2017.
16. "The use of the arboreal metaphor is precisely this goal: to build a pure and simple device of authority that, through contents evoked by the

image, feeds on semantic nuclei such as life, nature, biological necessity, hierarchy positions, and so on" (Bettini 2017: 34).

17. Finkielkraut 2013: 137.

18. In a similar nostalgic vein, the philosopher Michel Onfray exclaims: "The Judeo-Christian civilization is in a terminal phase" (Onfray 2017: 21), and a little further: "Decadence is a fact" (ibid.: 34). Onfray is wrong because the diagnosis of decadence, far from being a fact, usually occurs in the context of rising populism and nationalism. I refer here to the work of historian Michel Winock, who reminds us that "decadence is not a scientific concept" (Winock 2014: 127) and that its use "is never innocent" (ibid.: 35).

19. See McCormack 2017.

20. See https://theconversation.com/trumps-claim-that-europe-is-losing -its-culture-is-racism-and-it-must-be-challenged-99962.

21. For instance, in 2019, the new president-elect of the European Commission, Ursula von der Leyen, reframed the issue of migration, positioning it as a way to "protect the European way of life"—a phrase that is fraught with meaning and one that is employed frequently by the far right to stir up anxiety about the so-called cultural menace posed by migrants.

22. Talal Asad (2006), among others, has written about the "scarf controversy" in France, where the principle of *laïcité*, used as a feminist and secularist strategy to ban religious symbols from public institutions (schools, universities, administrations, etc.), has in fact contributed to feed discrimination against Muslims (and specifically Muslim women) in the general public.

23. Benjamin 2000: 433.

24. Honneth 1996.

25. See, for instance, Holsey (2008) and Urbain (2003).

26. Cunha 2010: 101.

27. But not always; see, e.g., Marlene Schäfers's text (2017) on Kurdish women who write about loss in a Turkey that does not recognize their traumatic history.

28. Mbembe 2013.

29. Altounian 2000; Epstein 2005.

30. Lapierre 2001: 31.

31. Perec 1995b.
32. On the brutal history of European colonial expansion, see the excellent volume edited by Marc Ferro (2010).
33. There is an abundance of literature, psychoanalytical in particular, on the experience of loss in traumatic situations, and the mechanisms of transmission involved in this type of scenario (Gampel 2005; Haddad 2011).
34. See the excellent book by Camille de Toledo (2009: 94).
35. The epigraph was published in 1842 in an essay significantly called "Avenir! Avenir!" (Future! Future!). It is cited by Benjamin 2000.
36. Foessel 2012: 7.
37. See *Le Monde*, 9/20/2013: http://www.lemonde.fr/idees/article/2013/09/20/bruno-latour-l-apocalypse-est-notre-chance_3481862_3232.html, an idea further discussed in a collective interview (Latour, Stengers, Tsing, and Bubandt 2018).
38. Le Breton 2002: 15.
39. Baumann 2017.
40. For a specific discussion of the feeling of loss in the context of environmental threats, read the remarkable article from Katharine Dow (2016).
41. The title of a work by David Lowenthal (1998).
42. Hérodote 1802: 1.
43. For a history of heritage-making in France, see, e.g., Poulot 2006.
44. Terdiman (1993) studies the historical context in which sciences of memory were developed from the mid-nineteenth century.
45. I draw inspiration from the work of Bendix 1997; Brantlinger 2003; Metcalf 2012; Rosaldo 1989; and L'Estoile 2007.
46. Lévi-Strauss 1961: 397.
47. For a recent discussion on episodic memory, I refer the reader to Mahr and Csibra (2017).
48. Landsberg 2004. A significant body of literature is dedicated to these "vicarious memories," in particular the persistence of traces of violent historical episodes. See, for example, the notion of "postmemory" forged by Marianne Hirsch (2012) to capture those traumatic memories of events that we did not experience personally. I believe that, in this context, the use of the concept of "memory" is inappropriate, as it tends

to bundle together a great diversity of psychosocial mechanisms under the same term (Berliner 2005a). Strictly speaking, we cannot remember situations that we did not experience. On the other hand, one can *know* things about this past, and identify with it. In this case, what is transmitted is a stock of emotionally loaded knowledge acquired through intergenerational interactions. I agree with Van Alphen's suggestion (2006) that the usage of the notion of memory serves to obscure the complexity of intergenerational processes.

49. More on this subject in Berliner and Bortolotto 2013 and Brumann and Berliner 2016.

50. An old problem already reported by Vine Deloria (1969) when denouncing the ways in which Native Americans are described by anthropologists as "losing their identity."

51. Sapir 1969: 91. Translator's translation.

52. Ethologists and primatologists are also interested in the mechanisms of cultural transmission in the animal world. See, among many others, Tomasello 2001 and Morin 2011.

53. I discuss this at length in Berliner 2010a.

54. Tylor 1994b: 401. According to him, survivals that had to be abandoned in light of the triumphant advent of reason, but which bore witness above all to the evidence itself of the "permanence in culture" (Tylor 1994a: 63). On this topic, it should be noted that Tylor's ambition was to describe the doctrine of animism and demonstrate "its transmission along the lines of religious thought" (Tylor 1994b: 326).

55. In *The Cultural Background of Personality*, published in 1945, Ralph Linton describes culture as "the configuration of learned behavior and results of behavior whose component elements are shared and transmitted by the members of a particular society" (Linton 1945a: 32) a point of view shared by Alfred Louis Kroeber and Clyde Kluckhohn, which gave rise to that most famous of definitions, according to which "culture consists of patterns, explicit and implicit, of and for behavior acquired and transmitted by symbols" (Kroeber and Kluckhohn 1952: 357). In the 1950s, from an English perspective and in a very different style, Alfred Reginald Radcliffe-Brown (1952: 5) suggests that "it is by reason of the existence of culture and cultural traditions that human social life differs very markedly from the social life of other animal

species," specifically by the fact that "transmission of learnt ways of thinking, feeling and acting constitutes the cultural process, which is a specific feature of human social life." From which came, to return to the American culturalist school of thought, Geertz's well-known definition of culture: "a historically transmitted pattern of meanings embodied in symbols, a system of inherited conceptions expressed in symbolic forms by means of which men communicate, perpetuate, and develop their knowledge about and attitudes toward life" (Geertz 1973: 89). To which we could add the examples of the founding texts, which all put emphasis on the fact that culture is transmitted (not by biological mechanisms, but by teaching and education), and transmission must therefore contribute to the perpetuation of the cultural.

56. Mauss 1968: 115.
57. Pouillon 1991: 710.
58. Hobsbawm 1983: 1.
59. See Latour 2006.
60. See Robbins 2007.
61. Radcliffe-Brown 1952: 10.
62. Bourdieu 1972.
63. Barth 1987.
64. Sahlins 1981.
65. Goody 1977.
66. Descola 2005.
67. Quoted in Jeudy 1990: 4.
68. On the subject of the transference of knowledge, Carlo Séveri (2015: 332) aptly remarks that the "form taken by such transmissions of knowledge usually attracts less interest." In his introduction to *The Naturalness of Religious Ideas*, Pascal Boyer (1994 : x) demonstrates his own surprise: "More complex, and not really understood at all, are the processes that underpin cultural transmission." New naturalist approaches moving into the field of cognitive science (Bloch 1998, 2005; Boyer 1994; Whitehouse 2004) have served to reinvigorate anthropological interest in the phenomena of cultural transmission.
69. Combining qualitative and quantitative methods can prove valuable. For the interested reader, see Schönpflug 2009 and Ellen, Lycett, and Johns 2013.

70. Bourdieu 1972: 94.

71. Candau 1998: 115.

72. The anthropological approach to time has been the subject of much discussion (Gell 1992). For recent analyses, see Jane Guyer on capitalist and evangelical temporalities in the United States (2007), and Laura Bear (2014) about "modern time."

73. See Naumescu 2010.

74. See Meyer 1998.

75. Scholem 1941: 329–330.

76. See Taussig 1993.

77. See Stoller 1995.

78. See Bhabha 1994.

79. Memmi 2013: 168.

80. For example, in 1930, Georges Hardy, the head of a colonial school, wrote: "There is . . . what I would call a risk of endosmosis, that is the quiet influence exercised upon the European of certain regrettable tendencies of the native environment, the erosion of certain scruples when in contact with a morality different to our own" (quoted in Saada 2005: 11).

81. See Nader 1970.

82. This notion of "plasticity" has become a paradigmatic trope in the field of brain studies. It enables us to consider the dynamic character of our thought processes and, in particular, to demonstrate how neurons are permanently altered by the experience (Ansermet and Magistretti 2011). See too Catherine Malabou's philosophical use of the concept (2005).

1. Transmission Impossible in West Africa

1. Those whom ethnologists, historians, art historians, linguists, and Guineans themselves typically refer to as "Baga" actually correspond to several different groups of rice farmers spread along the Guinean coast, from the Conakry Peninsula up to the Rio Componi (River Kogon). The Baga constitute seven subgroups, including the Bulongic, with whom I conducted my ethnographic fieldwork.

2. The power of objects to evoke certain images of the past, such as Proust's famous madeleine, should not be underestimated. Yet this

tendency to install memory *within* objects is also woven into the very particular fabric of our own history. Drawing inspiration from the works of historian Frances Yates, Küchler reminds us (Forty and Küchler 1999) of the memorization techniques dating back to the European Middle Ages (the *ars memorandi* used mental images based on objects or places for learning lengthy texts or poems by heart) to grasp our irresistible urge to think of objects as reassuring spaces for our memories, and to convince us that what is material is always, a priori, more memorable than what is not. In the field of anthropology (but also archaeology, museology, and other heritage-related sciences), it is this "objectification of memory" paradigm that, now more than ever, fuels the interest of researchers, leading to focus on the dominant roles of artifacts in processes of memory and identity (Hoskins 1998; Radley 1990). For a critical examination of the use of the concept of "material memory," see Berliner 2007.

3. I would refer any interested readers to an exhibition catalogue (Berliner 2013a) and a series of detailed ethnographic articles I devoted specifically to religion in this region of Guinea (Berliner 2005b; Berliner 2005c; Berliner 2007; Berliner 2008).

4. See Bravmann 1974.

5. Paulme 1958: 407.

6. See Theodossopoulos 2016a.

7. Nora 1977: 227.

8. Williams 1993: 7.

9. For a somehow comparable case, see Tuzin 1997 on the disappearance of Tambaran cults in Papua New Guinea.

10. See Zempléni 1976.

11. For a detailed description of this process, see my article, Berliner (2005b).

12. For comparison, see Borofsky 1987.

13. In 2005, the Kankurang initiation rituals of Senegal were added to the List of Intangible Cultural Heritage (UNESCO), a recognition that caused local tensions regarding the visibility of secrets. On this fascinating case study, see Ferdinand De Jong 2013.

14. Camara 1988: 1.

15. Ibid.

16. Ibid.: 3.
17. Ibid.: 6.
18. Ibid.: 8.
19. Ibid.: 9.
20. Ibid.: 16.

2. UNESCO, Bureaucratic Nostalgia, and Cultural Loss

1. I have especially been influenced by the work of Heinich 2009; Jeudy 2001; Hartog 2003; Nora 1977; and Thompson 1979.
2. Perec 2003: 163.
3. In his conference on "espaces autres" (other spaces) in Tunis in 1967, Foucault wrote: "Out of all these places that are distinct from one another, there are some that are completely different: ones that stand in contrast to all others, that are meant in some way to erase them, to neutralize them or to purify them. They are in a way counter-spaces. . . . Long before children did, adult society created its own 'counter-spaces,' these fixed utopias, real places away from all other places. Take, for example, gardens, cemeteries, asylums, brothels, Club Med villages and many more" (Foucault 2009: 24–25).
4. Ibid.: 30.
5. See Bortolotto 2007, 2013; Hafstein 2007; Brumann 2013, 2016; Labadi 2013; Meskell 2012, 2018; and Nielsen 2013.
6. See Brumann 2012 about the methodological intricacies of doing research about/with UNESCO experts.
7. For example, when it first began, UNESCO espoused an evolutionist "anti-superstition" stance (Stoczkowski 2009). With time, its scope has considerably widened to embrace ever more "relativist" and "postmodern" inclinations, notably with the adoption of the Convention for the Safeguarding of Intangible Cultural Heritage in 2003 (Bortolotto 2011).
8. There is a rich, rapidly growing literature about UNESCO heritage-making impacts. Among others, see Avieli 2015; Berliner and Istasse 2013; Byrne 2014; Ciarcia 2006; Meskell 2016, 2018; Probst 2016; Salazar 2016; Shepherd 2006; Wang 2016; Winter 2007; Owens 2002.
9. Jeudy 2001: 11.

10. Debray 1997: 20.
11. See especially Stuart-Fox 1997.
12. See Ivarrson 2008.
13. Perec 1995: 84.
14. UNESCO 2004.
15. See Nielsen 2013 on the bureaucratic pragmatism of UNESCO officials.
16. For anthropological theorization about expertise, see Boyer 2005.
17. Heinich 2009: 76.
18. See Herzfeld 1991.
19. A point of view not shared by many of the monks according to Suntikul 2009.
20. See http://www.lefigaro.fr/lefigaromagazine/2006/05/06/01006 -20060506ARTMAG90105-sortilges_de_luang_prabang.php.
21. See https://www.lemonde.fr/idees/article/2010/12/24/luang-prabang -peril-au-paradis_1457457_3232.html.
22. About tourists' motivations, see Caton and Santos 2007.
23. Peleggi 2002.
24. Evans 1998: 123.
25. To borrow Gayle Rubin's term (1975).
26. Evans 1998: 85–86.
27. *Vientiane Times*, February 29, 2008
28. According to tradition, Kabilaphom, the four-faced god known for his omniscience, challenged anyone to successfully answer his riddle. A young man, Thammabane Koumane, found the answer, and Kabila- phom ordered his own head to be cut off, a head possessing magical properties, which his seven daughters were thenceforth charged with anointing each year.
29. On the Internet, there are many forums for gay hookups in Luang Prabang. See, for instance, https://sawatdeenetwork.com/v4/archive /index.php/t-14219.html.
30. http://www.guscairns.com/Laos.htm.
31. See especially Lyttleton 2008. This tourism is not exclusively sexual in nature, and for many it is based on the desire to vacation in a "gay- friendly" location where they can feel at ease with their sexual identity. For a reflection on these questions, see Jaurand and Leroy 2010.

32. Brennan 2004: 709.

33. During the nineteenth century, European colonization was accompanied by the particular sexualization of colonized bodies and colonial spaces (Schick 1999), a favorite theme recurrent in literature of the time (Stoler 2002). Frank Proschan laid out the two tropes that appear regularly throughout: the hypersexualization of Asian women as sex-starved libertines, and the feminization of local men, seen as "androgynous, effeminate, hermaphroditic, impotent, and inverted" (Proschan 2002: 436). He argues that this kind of cliché is what afforded Europeans "a certain license to engage in homosexual relations" (ibid.: 442).

34. See Norindr 1997.

35. This was an unreferenced magazine of the kind one usually finds displayed in hotel lounges.

36. See, in particular, Jackson 1999.

37. While, in certain aspects, Luang Prabang constitutes a sexual heterotopia for gay tourists and expatriates, there are also many men in town who, without being transvestites or gays, sometimes even married, secretly have sex with other men, whether for pleasure or out of curiosity. According to Chris Lyttleton, in Vientiane, one in five men has confessed to having slept with another man at least once in his life (Lyttleton 2008). Far from the gay paradise of expatriates and tourists, these kinds of encounters do not take place in the town's gay bars and clubs, but rather in the dormitories of universities and factories, army barracks, countryside restaurants, and even temples, places of sexual education and socialization for young men discovering sex and practicing with other men (Berliner and Herbrand 2010). These meetings are shrouded in silence and secrecy, a dissimulation of homosexual behavior that makes it tolerable in a society in which such material and symbolic constraints relating to heteronormative gender and sexuality exist.

38. Evans 1998.

39. Long and Sweet 2006: 455.

40. See Koselleck 2004.

41. See Rethmann 2008.

42. Evans 1998: 122.

43. Fabre 2009: 44.

3. Toward the End of Societies?

1. Malinowski 1989: 52.
2. MacCarthy 2013: 2.
3. See an interview about her current research project at https://www
.uregina.ca/external/communications/feature-stories/current/2016/02
-22.html.
4. A concept borrowed from Taussig 1984.
5. For interested readers, see articles by Pap Ndiaye, Alastair Davidson,
Jacques Poloni-Simard, and Elikia M'Bokolo in Ferro (2010).
6. For a better understanding of this kind of diversity, see Barth et al. 2005.
7. See High 2011.
8. See Marcus and Fischer 1999.
9. See, e.g., Scheper-Hughes 1995.
10. For a critique of the use of "nostalgia" in social sciences, see Lankauskas 2014.
11. See, e.g., Boym 2001; Jameson 1991.
12. "Le paradigme des derniers." The notion was coined by Fabre (2008).
13. See the full interview at http://www.alanmacfarlane.com/ancestors
/richards.html.
14. See Metcalf 2002.
15. Mauss 1968: 119.
16. Ibid.: 144.
17. Lévy-Bruhl 2010: 563.
18. Spencer 2002: 71.
19. Lévi-Strauss 1975: 100.
20. Lévy-Bruhl 2010: 552.
21. Ibid.
22. Ibid.: 553.
23. Although, at the end of his life, he did express dissatisfaction with his
own antihistorical positions; see Kuper 2000.
24. Evans-Pritchard 1951: 9.
25. Quoted by Metcalf 2002: 118.
26. Sapir 1966: 96–97.
27. Here we find the persistence of evolutionist thinking and the influence
of Darwinism. From the nineteenth century on, the idea that inferior

beings would end up disappearing pervaded socio-Darwinist literature, "evidence of a state of humanity overtaken by European races and destined to disappear in the name of progress" (Pichot 2000: 141). For declinist thinkers, such as Georges Vacher de Lapouge and Arthur de Gobineau, the miscegenation was the source of degeneration, and the extinction of races was thus "naturalized" (ibid.: 356). Of course, considerable efforts were made by early anthropologists to abandon the swamp of Darwinism, in particular among followers of Boas. But it cannot be denied that, years later, socio-Darwinism does continue to inform their discourses on the persistence and disappearance of cultures.

28. Sarró 2009.

29. Jankélévitch 1974: 154.

30. Ibid.: 177.

31. Ibid.: 187.

32. See especially Karp and Lavine 1990.

33. Warnier 2007: 92.

34. See Herskovits 1956.

35. Capone 2005: 27.

36. Bastide 1970: 87.

37. Ibid.: 88.

38. Højbjerg 2007.

39. Knauft 1996: 133.

40. Ibid.

41. See Wachtel 2011.

42. See Stoller 1995.

43. Højbjerg 2002: 63.

44. I develop this idea in Berliner 2005a.

45. Shaw 2002: 264–265.

46. Ibid.: 268.

47. For instance, Antze and Lambek 1996.

48. Lambek 2002: 13.

49. Ibid.

50. Ibid.: 161.

51. See Sahlins 1981.

52. See Carsten 1995.

53. Appadurai 2013: 285.

54. Aurégan 2001: 549.

55. *Nostalgia Isn't What It Used to Be* is the title of Simone Signoret's 1978 autobiography. Although the content of the book is an anecdotal description of the actress's life, its ironic title invites us to reflect on the dynamism of nostalgic postures across time.

56. See Ardener 1987.

57. See Theodossopoulos 2016a.

58. Gille 2010: 288.

59. Kuklick 2008: 5.

4. The Plastic Anthropologist

1. Lévi-Strauss 1955: 1217.

2. The epistemological capability of anthropologists to access other people's reality has been much debated. See, especially, Rosen 1995.

3. See Stoler 2002.

4. Fontaine 2001.

5. Malinowski 1989.

6. Powdermaker 1966: 112.

7. Ibid.: 171.

8. Ibid.: 115.

9. Ibid.: 222.

10. Evans-Pritchard 1973: 3.

11. Ibid.

12. Leiris 1932: 433.

13. Ibid.: 423.

14. Ibid.: 436.

15. Favret-Saada 1977.

16. Scheper-Hughes 1995, among many others.

17. Wacquant 2010: 117.

18. From Stoller 2009.

19. Tedlock 1991: 82.

20. MacClancy 2005.

21. Another highly discussed question by anthropologists. See, e.g., Halloy 2007.

22. Declerck 2002.

23. Bourgois 1998.

24. Wacquant 2010: 116.

25. Ibid.

26. Ibid.: 121.

27. Allison 1994: 30. For more examples of anthropologists speaking of their experience as participant observers, see Okely 2012.

28. Geertz 1973.

29. Bourgois 1998.

30. Csordas 2007.

31. Notably Favret-Saada, but also Stoller 2009.

32. Tomasello 2001.

33. De Waal 2011: 162.

34. For an example of an anthropologist conducting fieldwork with "repugnant" others, see Harding 1991.

35. Dias 2005: 6.

36. Morin 2011: 67.

37. Bourgois 1998: 43.

38. Declerck 2001: 44.

39. Ibid.: 64.

40. Wacquant 2002: 8.

41. Ibid.

42. Powdermaker 1966: 148.

43. Geertz 1992.

44. Sartre 1976: 94.

45. Ibid.

46. Evans-Pritchard 1973: 4.

47. Ibid.

48. Ibid.

49. Garfinkel 2007: 242.

50. Ibid.

51. Declerck 2002.

52. Grossman 2008: 37.

53. Evans-Pritchard 1973: 4.

54. Powdermaker 1966: 197.

55. Ibid.: 291.

56. Leiris 1932: 162.
57. Grossman 2008: 12.
58. This phrase is from Devereux 2009.
59. Powdermaker 1966: 289.
60. Ibid.
61. Ogien 2011: 40.
62. Good 1991.
63. Grossman 2008: 17.
64. Leiris 1932: 225.
65. Devereux 1980: 16.
66. Ibid.: 79.
67. Ibid.: 134.

Conclusion

1. See Gilroy 2010.
2. Derrida 1996: 78.
3. For a discussion of these questions within the field of anthropology and the risk of ghettoization for our discipline, see Berliner 2008.
4. See especially Brumann 1999.
5. See, e.g., Berliner, Lambek, et al. 2016 and Berliner 2017.
6. Freud 1995: 88.
7. See, e.g., critiques by Todorov 1995 and Terray 2005.
8. Sec Lapierre 2007.
9. https://next.liberation.fr/cinema/2004/09/29/nankin-sous-le-choc-de-shoah_494158. About the creation of such "cosmopolitan memories," see Levy and Sznaider 2005.
10. See Rousso 2016.
11. About memory frictions, see an excellent piece by Shaw (2007).
12. The term is coined by Misztal 2004.
13. Ricoeur is an invaluable source to think through contemporary memory politics.
14. See Bishop 1984.
15. See Rieff 2018.
16. Benjamin 2011: 40.
17. See, in particular, Berliner 2018 and Milton 2002.

18. See Robertson 1992.

19. This was a territorial dispute dating back to the colonial era. In 1962, and again in 2013, the International Court of Justice ruled in favor of Cambodia, and as of 2014 there has been no further confrontation between the two countries over the matter. I refer the interested reader to the anthropological analyses of Silverman (2011).

20. Warnier 2007: 106.

21. See Butler 2013.

22. See Haraway 2016.

23. See Latour 2012.

24. For a discussion of Latour's contribution to anthropology, see Berliner, Van de Port, and Legrain 2013.

Bibliography

Allison, Anne. 1994. *Nightwork: Sexuality, Pleasure, and Corporate Masculinity in a Tokyo Hostess Club*. Chicago: University of Chicago Press.

Altounian, Janine. 2000. *La survivance: Traduire le trauma collectif.* Paris: Dunod.

Ange, Olivia. 2015. "Le goût d'autrefois: Pain au levain et attachements nostalgiques dans la société contemporaine." *Terrain* 65: 34–51.

Ange, Olivia, and David Berliner, eds. 2014. *Anthropology and Nostalgia*. New York: Berghahn Books.

Ansermet, François, and Pierre Magistretti. 2011. *A chacun son cerveau: Plasticité neuronale et inconscient*. Paris: Odile Jacob.

Antze, Paul, and Michael Lambek. 1996. *Tense Past: Cultural Essays in Trauma and Memory*. New York: Routledge.

Appadurai, Arjun. 1996. *Modernity at Large: Cultural Dimensions of Globalization*. Minneapolis: University of Minnesota Press.

———. 2013. *The Future as a Cultural Fact: Essays on the Global Condition*. London: Verso.

Ardener, Edwin. 1987. "'Remote Areas': Some Theoretical Considerations." In *Anthropology at Home*, edited by Anthony Jackson. ASA Monographs 25. London: Tavistock Publications.

Aristotle. 2010. *Poétique*. Paris: Mille et une nuits.

Asad, Talal. 2006. "Trying to Understand French Secularism." In *Political Theologies: Public Religions in a Post-Secular World*, edited by Hent de Vries and Lawrence Eugene Sullivan. New York: Fordham University Press.

Aurégan, Pierre. 2001. *Terre humaine, des récits et des hommes: Un autre regard sur les sciences de l'homme*. Paris: Agora.

Avieli, Nir. 2015. "The Rise and Fall(?) of Hoi An, a UNESCO World Heritage Site in Vietnam." *Journal of Social Issues in Southeast Asia* 30 (1): 35–71.

Barth, Fredrik. 1987. *Cosmologies in the Making: A Generative Approach to Cultural Variation in Inner New Guinea.* Cambridge: Cambridge University Press.

Barth, Fredrik, Andre Gingrich, Robert Parkin, and Sydel Silverman. 2005. *One Discipline, Four Ways: British, German, French, and American Anthropology.* Chicago: University of Chicago Press.

Bartholeyns, G. 2014. "Nostalgia and Digital Retro Photography." In *Media and Nostalgia: Yearning for the Past, Present and Future*, edited by Katharina Niemeyer. London: Palgrave Macmillan.

Bastide, Roger. 1970. "Mémoire collective et sociologie du bricolage." *L'année sociologique (1940/1948)* 21: 65–108.

Baudelaire, Charles. 1869. *Oeuvres complètes de Charles Baudelaire.* Paris: Michel Lévy frères.

Bauman, Zygmunt. 2017. *Retrotopia.* Cambridge: Polity Press.

Bear, Laura. 2014. "Doubt, Conflict, Mediation: The Anthropology of Modern Time." *Journal of the Royal Anthropological Institute* 20 (1): 3–30.

Behar, Ruth. 2003. *Translated Woman: Crossing the Border with Esperanza's Story.* Boston: Beacon Press.

Bendix, Regina. 1997. *In Search of Authenticity: The Formation of Folklore Studies.* Madison: University of Wisconsin Press.

Benjamin, Walter. 2000. *Oeuvres.* Vol. 3. Paris: Gallimard.

———. 2011. *Expérience et pauvreté.* Paris: Editions Payot & Rivages.

Berliner, David. 2005a. "The Abuses of Memory: Reflections on the Memory Boom in Anthropology." *Anthropological Quarterly* 78 (1): 197–211.

———. 2005b. "La féminisation de la coutume." *Cahiers d'études africaines* 177 (April): 15–37.

———. 2005c. "An 'Impossible' Transmission: Youth Religious Memories in Guinea-Conakry." *American Ethnologist* 32 (4): 576–592.

———. 2007. "When the Object of Transmission Is Not an Object: A West African Example (Guinea-Conakry)." *RES: Anthropology and Aesthetics* 51: 87–97.

———. 2008. "The Anthropologist in the Middle of a Tug-of-War (Guinea-Conakry)." *Men and Masculinities* 11: 174–185.

———. 2009. "Memories of Initiation Violence: Remembered Pain and Religious Transmission in Guinea-Conakry." In *Remembering Violence: Study in Intergenerational Transmission*, edited by Nicolas Argenti and Katharina Schramm. Oxford: Berghahn Books.

———. 2010a. "Introduction: L'anthropologie et la transmission." *Terrain* 55: 3–15.

———. 2010b. "Perdre l'esprit du lieu." *Terrain* 55: 4–19.

———. 2012. "Multiple Nostalgias: The Fabric of Heritage in Luang Prabang (Lao PDR)." *Journal of the Royal Anthropological Institute* 18 (4): 769–786.

———. 2013a. *Baga: Mémoires religieuses*. Paris: Editions Somogy.

———. 2013b. "Le désir de participation ou comment jouer à être un autre." *L'homme* 206: 51–70.

———. 2013c. "Nostalgie et patrimoine: Une esquisse de typologie." In *Emotions patrimoniales*, edited by Daniel Fabre and Annick Arnaud. Paris: Editions de la Maison des sciences de l'homme.

———. 2013d. "New Directions in the Study of Cultural Transmission." In *Anthropological Perspectives on Intangible Cultural Heritage*, edited by Lourdes Arizpe and Cristina Amescua. Heidelberg: Springer.

———. 2014a. "Are Anthropologists Nostalgist?" In *Anthropology and Nostalgia*, edited by Olivia Angé and David Berliner. New York: Berghahn Books.

——— 2014b. "On Exonostalgia." *Anthropological Theory* 14 (4): 373–386.

———. 2017a. "Contradictions: From the Intrapersonal to the Social, and Back." *Hau Journal of Ethnographic Theory* 7 (2): 45–49.

———. 2017b. "Rendez-vous en terre (in)connue? Sur le mythe du bon sauvage à la télé." *La revue nouvelle* 1: 14–16.

———. 2018. "Can Anything Become Heritage?" In *Sense and Essence: Heritage and the Cultural Production of the Real*, edited by Birgit Meyer and Mattijs Van de Port. Oxford: Berghahn Books.

Berliner, David, and Chiara Bortolotto. 2013. "Introduction: Le monde selon l'Unesco." *Gradhiva* 18 (December): 4–21.

Berliner, David, and Cathy Herbrand. 2010. "Sexualités: Apprentissages et Performances." *Civilisations. Revue internationale d'anthropologie et de sciences humaines* 59 (1): 2–11.

Berliner, David, and Manon Istasse. 2013. "Les hyper-lieux du patrimoine mondial." *Gradhiva* 18 (December): 124–145.

Berliner, David, Michael Lambek, Richard Shweder, Richard Irvine, and Albert Piette. 2016. "Anthropology and the Study of Contradictions." *Hau: Journal of Ethnographic Theory* 6 (1): 1–27.

Berliner, David, Mattjis Van de Port, and Laurent Legrain. 2013. "Latour and the Anthropology of the Moderns." *Social Anthropology/Anthropologie sociale* 21 (4): 1–27.

Bettini, Maurizio. 2017. *Contre les racines*. Paris: Flammarion.

Bhabha, Homi. 1994. *The Location of Culture*. London: Routledge.

Bishop, Elizabeth. 1984. *The Complete Poems, 1927–1979*. New York: Farrar, Straus & Giroux.

Bloch, Maurice. 1998. *How We Think They Think: Approaches to Cognition, Memory, and Literacy*. Oxford: Westview Press.

———. 2005. *Essays on Cultural Transmission*. London: Berg.

Borofsky, Robert. 1987. *Making History: Pukapukan and Anthropological Constructions of Knowledge*. Cambridge: Cambridge University Press.

Bortolotto, Chiara. 2007. "From Objects to Processes: UNESCO's Intangible Cultural Heritage." *Journal of Museum Ethnography* 19: 21–33.

———. 2011. *Le patrimoine culturel immatériel: Enjeux d'une nouvelle catégorie*. Vol. 26. Paris: Éditions de la Maison des sciences de l'homme.

———. 2013. "L'Unesco comme arène de traduction: La fabrique globale du patrimoine immatériel." *Gradhiva* 18 (December): 50–73.

Bourdieu, Pierre. 1972. *Esquisse d'une théorie de la pratique: Précédé de trois études d'ethnologie kabyle*. Geneva: Droz.

Bourgois, Philippe. 1998. "Just Another Night in a Shooting Gallery." *Theory, Culture & Society* 15 (2): 37–66.

———. 2003. *In Search of Respect: Selling Crack in El Barrio*. Cambridge: Cambridge University Press.

Boyer, Dominic. 2005. "The Corporeality of Expertise." *Ethnos* 70 (2): 243–266.

Boyer, Pascal. 1994. *The Naturalness of Religious Ideas: A Cognitive Theory of Religion*. Berkeley and Los Angeles, CA: University of California Press.

Boym, Svetlana. 2001. *The Future of Nostalgia*. New York: Basic Books.

Brantlinger, Patrick. 2003. *Dark Vanishings: Discourse on the Extinction of Primitive Races, 1800–1930*. Ithaca, NY: Cornell University Press.

Bravmann, René. 1974. *Islam and Tribal Art in West Africa*. London: Cambridge University Press.

Brennan, Denise. 2004. "Women Work, Men Sponge, and Everyone Gossips: Macho Men and Stigmatized/ing Women in a Sex Tourist Town." *Anthropological Quarterly* 77 (4): 705–733.

Brumann, Christoph. 1999. "Writing for Culture: Why a Successful Concept Should Not Be Discarded." *Current Anthropology* 40 (1): 1–27.

———. 2012. *Multilateral Ethnography: Entering the World Heritage Arena*. Halle: Max Planck Institute for Social Anthropology.

———. 2013. "Comment le patrimoine mondial de l'Unesco devient immatériel." *Gradhiva* 18 (December): 22–49.

———. 2016. "Imagining the Ground from Afar: Why the Sites Are So Remote in World Heritage Committee Sessions." In *World Heritage on the Ground: Ethnographic Perspectives*, edited by Christoph Brumann and David Berliner. Oxford: Berghahn Books.

Brumann, Christoph, and David Berliner. 2016. *World Heritage on the Ground: Ethnographic Perspectives*. Oxford: Berghahn Books.

Butler, Judith. 2013. *Vers la cohabitation: Judéité et critique du sionisme*. Paris: Fayard.

Byrne, Denis. 2014. *Counterheritage: Critical Perspectives on Heritage Conservation in Asia*. New York: Routledge.

Camara, Ibrahima. 1988. "Traditionalisme Baga." Conakry. Unpublished.

Candau, Joël. 1998. *Mémoire et identité*. Paris: Presses universitaires de France.

Capone, Stefania. 2005. *Les Yoruba du Nouveau Monde: Religion, ethnicité et nationalisme noir aux Etats-Unis*. Paris: Karthala.

Carsten, Janet. 1995. "The Politics of Forgetting: Migration, Kinship and Memory on the Periphery of the Southeast Asian State." *Journal of the Royal Anthropological Institute* 1 (2): 317–335.

Cassin, Barbara. 2013. *La nostalgie: Quand donc est-on chez soi?* Paris: Editions Autrement.

Caton, Kellee, and Carla Almeida Santos. 2007. "Heritage Tourism on Route 66: Deconstructing Nostalgia." *Journal of Travel Research* 45 (4): 371–386.

Ciarcia, Gaetano. 2006. *La perte durable: Etude sur la notion de "patrimoine immatériel."* Mission Ethnologie (Ministère de la Culture). https:// halshs.archives-ouvertes.fr/halshs-00505583/document.

Comaroff, John, and Jean Comaroff. 2018. *The Politics of Custom: Chiefship, Capital, and the State in Contemporary Africa.* Chicago: University of Chicago Press.

Cross, Gary. 2015. *Consumed Nostalgia: Memory in the Age of Fast Capitalism.* New York: Columbia University Press.

Csordas, Thomas J. 2007. "Transmutation of Sensibilities: Empathy, Intuition, Revelation." In *The Shadow Side of Fieldwork,* edited by Athena McLean and Annette Leibing. Oxford: Blackwell Publishing.

Cunha, Manuela Carneiro da. 2010. *Savoir traditionnel, droits intellectuels et dialectique de la culture.* Paris: Editions de l'éclat.

Davis, Fred. 1979. *Yearning for Yesterday: A Sociology of Nostalgia.* New York: Free Press.

Debray, Régis. 1997. *Transmettre.* Paris: Odile Jacob.

Declerck, Patrick. 2001. *Les naufragés: Avec les clochards de Paris.* Paris: Plon.

———. 2002. Interview with Patrick Declerck. *No Pasaran 6.* http:// nopasaran.samizdat.net/spip.php?article20.

De Jong, Ferdinand. 2013. "Le secret exposé: Révélation et reconnaissance d'un patrimoine immatériel au Sénégal." *Gradhiva* 18: 98–123.

Deloria, Vine. 1969. *Custer Died for Your Sins: An Indian Manifesto.* New York: Macmillan.

Derrida, Jacques. 1996. "Un témoignage donné . . ." In *Questions au judaïsme: Entretiens avec Elisabeth Weber,* edited by Elisabeth Weber. Paris: Desclée de Brouwer.

———. 2014. *Le dernier des Juifs.* Paris: Editions Galilée.

Descola, Philippe, 2005. *Par-delà nature et culture.* Paris: Flammarion.

de Toledo, Camille. 2009. *Le hêtre et le bouleau: Essai sur la tristesse européenne.* Paris: Editions Le Seuil.

Devereux, Georges. 1980. *De l'angoisse à la méthode dans les sciences du comportement.* Paris: Flammarion.

———. 2009. *La renonciation à l'identité.* Paris: Payot.

De Waal, Frans. 2011. *L'âge de l'empathie: Leçons de la nature pour une société solidaire.* Arles: Actes Sud.

Diamond, Jared. 2013. *Le monde jusqu'à hier: Ce que nous apprennent les sociétés traditionnelles*. Paris: Gallimard.

Dias, Nélia. 2005. "Imitation et anthropologie." *Terrain* 44 (March): 5–18.

Dow, Katharine. 2016. "What Gets Left behind for Future Generations? Reproduction and the Environment in Spey Bay, Scotland." *Journal of the Royal Anthropological Institute* 22: 653–669.

Ellen, Roy, Stephen Lycett, and Sarah Johns. 2013. *Understanding Cultural Transmission in Anthropology: A Critical Synthesis*. Oxford: Berghahn Books.

Epstein, Helen. 2005. *Le traumatisme en héritage: Conversations avec des fils et filles de survivants de la Shoah*. Paris: La cause des livres.

Ernaux, Annie. 2008. *Les années*. Paris: Gallimard.

Evans, Grant. 1998. *The Politics of Ritual and Remembrance: Laos since 1975*. Honolulu: University of Hawai'i Press.

Evans-Pritchard, E. E. 1951. *Social Anthropology*. London: Cohen & West.

———. 1973. "Some Reflections and Reminiscences on Fieldwork." *Journal of the Anthropological Society of Oxford* 4 (1): 1–13.

Fabre, Daniel. 2008. "Chinoiserie des Lumières: Variations sur l'individu-monde." *L'homme* 185–186: 269–299.

———. 2009. "Habiter les monuments." In *Les monuments sont habités*, edited by Daniel Fabre and Anna Iuso. Paris: Editions de la Maison des sciences de l'homme.

Favret-Saada, Jeanne. 1977. *Les mots, la mort, les sorts*. Paris: Gallimard.

Ferro, Marc, ed. 2010. *Le livre noir du colonialisme: XVIe–XXIe siècle, De l'extermination à la repentance*. Paris: Fayard.

Finkielkraut, Alain. 2013. *L'identité malheureuse*. Paris: Gallimard.

Foessel, Michaël. 2012. *Après la fin du monde: Critique de la raison apocalyptique*. Paris: Editions Le Seuil.

Fontaine, Dorothy. 2001. "Going Native in the Twentieth Century." Unpublished doctoral thesis, Rice University.

Forty, Adrian, and Susanne Küchler. 1999. *The Art of Forgetting*. Oxford: Berg.

Foucault, Michel. 2009. *Le corps utopique: Suivi de Les hétérotopies*. Paris: Nouvelles éditions Lignes.

Freud, Sigmund. 1995. *Le malaise dans la culture*. Paris: Presses universitaires de France.

Fukuyama, Francis. 1992. *La fin de l'histoire et le dernier homme*. Paris: Flammarion.

Gampel, Yolande. 2005. *Ces parents qui vivent à travers moi: Les enfants des guerres*. Paris: Fayard.

Garfinkel, Harold. 2007. *Recherches en ethnométhodologie*. Paris: Presses universitaires de France.

Geertz, Clifford. 1973. *The Interpretation of Cultures: Selected Essays*. New York: Basic Books.

———. 1992. *Ici et là-bas: L'anthropologue comme auteur*. Paris: Editions Métailié.

Gell, Alfred. 1992. *The Anthropology of Time: Cultural Constructions of Temporal Maps and Images*. London: Berg.

Gille, Zsuzsa. 2010. "Postscript." In *Post-Communist Nostalgia*, edited by Maria Nikolaeva Todorova and Zsuzsa Gille. Oxford: Berghahn Books.

Gilroy, Paul. 2010. *L'Atlantique noir: Modernité et double conscience*. Paris: Editions Amsterdam.

Good, Kenneth. 1991. *Into the Heart: One Man's Pursuit of Love and Knowledge among the Yanomama*. New York: Simon & Schuster.

Goody, Jack. 1977. "Mémoire et apprentissage dans les sociétés avec et sans écriture: La transmission du Bagré." *L'homme* 17 (1): 29–52.

Grossman, Évelyne. 2008. *L'angoisse de penser*. Paris: Editions de Minuit.

Guyer, Jane. 2007. "Prophecy and the Near Future: Thoughts on Macroeconomic, Evangelical, and Punctuated Time." *American Ethnologist* 34 (3): 409–421.

Haddad, Gérard. 2011. *Lumière des astres éteints: La psychanalyse face au camp*. Paris: Grasset.

Hafstein, Valdimar. 2007. "Claiming Culture: Intangible Heritage Inc., Folklore©, Traditional Knowledge™." In *Prädikat "Heritage": Wertschöpfungen aus kulturellen Ressourcen*, edited by Dorothee Hemme, Markus Tauschek, and Regina Bendix. Berlin: Lit.

Haley, Alex. 1977. *Racines*. Paris: Editions J'ai lu.

Halloy, Arnaud. 2007. "Un anthropologue en transe: Du corps comme outils d'investigation ethnographique." In *Corps, performance, religion: Etudes anthropologiques offertes à Philippe Jespers*, edited by Joël Noret and Pierre Petit. Paris: Publibook.com.

Haraway, Donna Jeanne. 2016. *Staying with the Trouble: Making Kin in the Chthulucene.* Durham, NC: Duke University Press.

Harding, Susan. 1991. "Representing Fundamentalism: The Problem of the Repugnant Cultural Other." *Social Research* 58 (2): 373–393.

Hartog, François. 2003. *Régimes d'historicité: Présentisme et expériences du temps.* Paris: Editions du Seuil.

Heinich, Nathalie. 2009. *La fabrique du patrimoine: De la cathédrale à la petite cuillère.* Paris: Editions de la Maison des sciences de l'homme.

Hérodote. 1802. *Histoire d'Hérodote.* Paris: G. Debure l'aîné.

Herskovits, Melville J. 1956. *Man and His Works: The Science of Cultural Anthropology.* New York: A. A. Knopf.

Herzfeld, Michael. 1991. *A Place in History: Social and Monumental Time in a Cretan Town.* Princeton, NJ: Princeton University Press.

———. 2007. *L'intimité culturelle: Poétique sociale de l'état nation.* Québec: Presses de l'Université Laval.

High, Holly. 2011. "Melancholia and Anthropology." *American Ethnologist* 38 (2): 217–233.

Hirsch, Marianne. 2012. *The Generation of Postmemory: Writing and Visual Culture after the Holocaust.* New York: Columbia University Press.

Hobsbawm, Eric. 1983. "Introduction: Inventing Traditions." In *The Invention of Tradition*, edited by E. Hobsbawm and T. Ranger. Cambridge: Cambridge University Press.

Højbjerg, Christian. 2002. "Inner Iconoclasm: Forms of Reflexivity in Loma Rituals of Sacrifice." *Social Anthropology* 10 (1): 57–75.

———. 2007. *Resisting State Iconoclasm among the Loma of Guinea.* Durham, NC: Carolina Academic Press.

Holsey, Bayo. 2008. *Routes of Remembrance: Refashioning the Slave Trade in Ghana.* Chicago: The University of Chicago Press.

Honneth, Axel. 1996. *The Struggle for Recognition.* Cambridge, MA: MIT Press.

Hoskins, Janet. 1998. *Biographical Objects: How Things Tell the Stories of People's Lives.* New York: Routledge.

Ivarsson, Søren. 2008. *Creating Laos: The Making of a Lao Space between Indochina and Siam, 1860–1945.* Copenhagen: NIAS Press.

Jackson, Peter A. 1999. "Tolerant but Unaccepting: The Myth of a Thai 'Gay Paradise.'" In *Genders and Sexualities in Modern Thailand*, edited by Peter A. Jackson and Nerida M. Cook. Chiang Mai, Thailand: Silkworm Books.

Jameson, F. 1991. *Postmodernism, or, The Cultural Logic of Late Capitalism.* Durham, NC: Duke University Press.

Jankélévitch, Vladimir. 1974. *L'irréversible et la nostalgie.* Paris: Flammarion.

Jaurand, Emmanuel, and Stéphane Leroy. 2010. "Le tourisme gay: Aller ailleurs pour être soi-même?" EspacesTemps.net, February. http://www .espacestemps.net/document8000.html.

Jeudy, Henry-Pierre. 1990. *Patrimoines en folie.* Paris: Editions de la Maison des sciences de l'homme.

———. 2001. *La machinerie patrimoniale.* Paris: Sens & Tonka.

Karp, Ivan, and Steven Lavine, eds. 1990. *Exhibiting Cultures: The Poetics and Politics of Museum Display.* Washington, DC: Smithsonian Institution Press.

Knauft, Bruce M. 1996. *Genealogies for the Present in Cultural Anthropology.* New York: Routledge.

Koselleck, Reinhart. 2004. *Futures Past: On the Semantics of Historical Time.* New York: Columbia University Press.

Kroeber, Alfred, and Clyde Kluckhohn. 1952. *Culture: A Critical Review of Concepts and Definitions.* New York: Random House.

Kroeber, Theodora. 1964. *Ishi in Two Worlds: A Biography of the Last Wild Indian in North America.* Berkeley: University of California Press.

Kuklick, Henrika. 2008. *A New History of Anthropology.* Oxford: Blackwell Publishing.

Kuper, Adam. 2000. *Culture: The Anthropologists' Account.* Cambridge, MA: Harvard University Press.

Labadi, Sophia. 2013. *UNESCO, Cultural Heritage, and Outstanding Universal Value: Value-Based Analyses of the World Heritage and Intangible Cultural Heritage Conventions.* Lanham, MD: AltaMira Press.

Lambek, Michael. 2002. *The Weight of the Past: Living with History in Mahajanga, Madagascar.* Basingstoke: Palgrave Macmillan.

Landsberg, Alison. 2004. *Prosthetic Memory: The Transformation of American Remembrance in the Age of Mass Culture.* New York: Columbia University Press.

Lankauskas, Gediminas. 2014. "Missing Socialism Again? The Malaise of Nostalgia in Post-Soviet Lithuania." In *Anthropology and Nostalgia*, edited by Olivia Ange and David Berliner. Oxford: Berghahn Books.

Lapierre, Nicole. 2001. *Le silence de la mémoire: A la recherche des Juifs de Płock*. Paris: Le Livre de poche.

———. 2007. "Le cadre référentiel de la Shoah." *Ethnologie française* 37 (3): 475–482.

Latour, Bruno. 2006. *Changer de société: Refaire de la sociologie*. Paris: Editions de la Découverte.

———. 2012. *Enquête sur les modes d'existence: Une anthropologie des modernes*. Paris: Editions de la Découverte.

Latour, Bruno, Isabelle Stengers, Anna Tsing, and Nils Bubandt. 2018. "Anthropologists Are Talking—about Capitalism, Ecology and Apocalypse." *Ethnos* 83 (3): 587–606.

Le Breton, David. 2002. *Signes d'identité: Tatouages, piercings et autres marques corporelles*. Paris: Editions Métailié.

Le Goff, Jean-Pierre. 2012. *La fin du village: Une histoire française*. Paris: Gallimard.

Leiris, Michel. 1932. *L'Afrique fantôme*. Paris: Gallimard.

L'Estoile, Benoit de. 2007. *Le goût des autres: De l'exposition coloniale aux arts premiers*. Paris: Flammarion.

Lévi-Strauss, Claude. 1955. "Diogène couché." *Les temps modernes* 110: 1187–1220.

———. 1961. *A World on the Wane*. London: Criterion Books.

———. 1975. *Les sociétés primitives*. Paris: Grammont; Lausanne: R. Laffont.

Levy, Daniel, and Natan Sznaider. 2005. *Holocaust and Memory in the Global Age*. Philadelphia: Temple University Press.

Lévy-Bruhl, Lucien. 2010. *La mentalité primitive*. Paris: Flammarion.

Linton, Ralph. 1945a. *The Cultural Background of Personality*. New York: Appleton-Century-Crofts.

———. 1945b. *The Science of Man in the World Crisis*. New York: Columbia University Press.

Long, Colin, and Jonathan Sweet. 2006. "Globalization, Nationalism and World Heritage: Interpreting Luang Prabang." *South East Asia Research* 14 (3): 445–469.

Lowenthal, David. 1998. *The Heritage Crusade and the Spoils of History.* Cambridge: Cambridge University Press.

Lyttleton, Chris. 2008. *Mekong Erotics: Men Loving, Pleasuring, Using Men in Lao PDR.* Bangkok: UNESCO Asia and Pacific Regional Bureau for Education.

MacCarthy, Michelle. 2013. "'More Than Grass Skirts and Feathers': Negotiating Culture in the Trobriand Islands." *International Journal of Heritage Studies* 19 (1): 62–77.

MacClancy, Jeremy. 2005. "The Literary Image of Anthropologists." *Journal of the Royal Anthropological Institute* 11 (3): 549–575.

Mahr, Johannes, and Gergely Csibra. 2017. "Why Do We Remember? The Communicative Function of Episodic Memory." *Behavioral and Brain Sciences* 41: 1–93.

Malabou, Catherine. 2005. *La plasticité au soir de l'écriture: Dialectique, destruction, déconstruction.* Paris: Editions Léo Scheer.

Malinowski, Bronislaw. 1922. *Argonauts of the Western Pacific: An Account of Native Enterprise and Adventure in the Archipelagos of Melanesian New Guinea.* London: Routledge; New York: E. P. Dutton.

———. 1989 (1967). *A Diary in the Strict Sense of the Term.* Stanford: Stanford University Press.

Marcus, George E., and Michael M. J. Fischer. 1999. *Anthropology as Cultural Critique: An Experimental Moment in the Human Sciences.* Chicago: University of Chicago Press.

Mauss, Marcel. 1950 (1934). *Sociologie et anthropologie.* Paris: Presses universitaires de France.

———. 1968. *Essais de sociologie.* Paris: Editions de Minuit.

Mbembe, Achille. 2013. *Critique de la raison nègre.* Paris: Editions de la Découverte.

McCarthy, Tom. 2017. *Satin Island.* Paris: Les Editions de l'Olivier.

McCormack, Jo. 2017. "Narratives of Decline in Contemporary France: Nostalgia, Melancholy, and Selective Memory." In *Remembering Home in a Time of Mobility: Memory, Nostalgia and Melancholy,* edited by Maja Mikula. Newcastle upon Tyne: Cambridge Scholars.

Mead, Margaret. 1930. *Growing Up in New Guinea: A Comparative Study of Primitive Education.* New York: W. Morrow.

Memmi, Albert. 2013. *The Colonizer and the Colonized.* London: Routledge.

Meskell, Lynn. 2012. "The Rush to Inscribe: Reflections on the 35th Session of the World Heritage Committee, UNESCO Paris, 2011." *Journal of Field Archaeology* 37 (2): 145–151.

———. 2016. "Mapungubwe Cultural Landscape: Extractive Economies and Endangerment on South Africa's Borders." In *World Heritage on the Ground: Ethnographic Perspectives*, edited by Christoph Brumann and David Berliner. Oxford: Berghahn Books.

———. 2018. *A Future in Ruins: UNESCO, World Heritage, and the Dream of Peace*. Oxford: Oxford University Press.

Metcalf, Peter. 2002. *They Lie, We Lie: Getting on with Anthropology*. London: Routledge.

———. 2012. "Nostalgia and Neocolonialism." In *Returns to the Field: Multitemporal Research and Contemporary Anthropology*, edited by Signe Howell and Aud Talle. Bloomington: Indiana University Press.

Meyer, Birgit. 1998. "'Make a Complete Break with the Past': Memory and Post-Colonial Modernity in Ghanaian Pentecostalist Discourse." *Journal of Religion in Africa* 28(3): 316–349.

Milton, Kay. 2002. *Loving Nature*. London: Routledge.

Misztal, Barbara. 2004. "The Sacralization of Memory." *European Journal of Social Theory* 7 (1): 67–84.

Morin, Olivier. 2011. *Comment les traditions naissent et meurent: La transmission culturelle*. Paris: Odile Jacob.

Musil, Robert. 2004. *L'homme sans qualités*. Paris: Éditions Le Seuil.

Nader, Laura. 1970. "From Anguish to Exultation." In *Women in the Field: Anthropological Experiences*, edited by Peggy Golde. Berkeley: University of California Press.

Naumescu, Vlad. 2010. "Le vieil homme et le livre: La crise de la transmission chez les vieux-croyants (Roumanie)." *Terrain* 55: 72–89.

Nielsen, Bjarke. 2013. "L'Unesco et le culturellement correct." *Gradhiva* 18 (December): 74–97.

Niemeyer, Katharina. 2014. *Media and Nostalgia: Yearning for the Past, Present and Future*. London: Palgrave Macmillan.

Nora, Pierre. 1977. "Mémoire de l'historien, mémoire de l'histoire: Entretien avec J.-B. Pontalis." *Nouvelle revue de psychanalyse* 15: 221–232.

Norindr, P. 1997. *Phantasmatic Indochina: French Colonial Ideology in Architecture, Film, and Literature*. Durham, NC: Duke University Press.

Ogien, Ruwen. 2011. *L'influence de l'odeur des croissants chauds sur la bonté humaine et autres questions de philosophie morale expérimentale*. Paris: Grasset.

Okely, Judith. 2012. *Anthropological Practice: Fieldwork and the Ethnographic Method*. London: Bloomsbury Academic.

Onfray, Michel. 2017. *Décadence*. Paris: Flammarion.

Owens, Bruce McCoy. 2002. "Monumentality, Identity, and the State: Local Practice, World Heritage, and Heterotopia at Swayambhu, Nepal." *Anthropological Quarterly* 75 (2): 269–316.

Paulme, Denise. 1958. "La notion de sorcier chez les Baga." *Bulletin de l'Institut français d'Afrique noire. Série B, Sciences humaines* 20: 3–4.

Peleggi, Maurizio. 2002. *The Politics of Ruins and the Business of Nostalgia*. Bangkok: White Lotus Press.

Perec, Georges. 1995a. *Ellis Island*. Paris: P.O.L.

———. 1995b. *L'infra-ordinaire*. Paris: Editions Le Seuil.

———. 2003. *Penser/Classer*. Paris: Editions Le Seuil.

Pichot, André. 2000. *La société pure: De Darwin à Hitler*. Paris: Flammarion.

Pouillon, Jean. 1991. "Tradition." In *Dictionnaire de l'ethnologie et de l'anthropologie*, edited by P. Bonte and M. Izard. Paris: Presses universitaires de France.

Poulot, Dominique. 2006. *Une histoire du patrimoine en Occident, XVIIIe–XXIe siècle: Du monument aux valeurs*. Paris: Presses universitaires de France.

Powdermaker, Hortense. 1966. *Stranger and Friend: The Way of an Anthropologist*. New York: W. W. Norton.

Probst, Peter. 2016. "The Values of Exchange and the Issue of Control: Living with (World) Heritage in Osogbo, Nigeria." In *World Heritage on the Ground: Ethnographic Perspectives*, edited by Christoph Brumann and David Berliner. Oxford: Berghahn Books.

Proschan, Frank. 2002. "Eunuch Mandarins, Soldats Mamzelles, Effeminate Boys, and Graceless Women: French Colonial Constructions of Vietnamese Genders." *GLQ: A Journal of Lesbian and Gay Studies* 8 (4): 435–467.

Radcliffe-Brown, Alfred. 1952. *Structure and Function in Primitive Society*. London: Cohen and West.

Radley, Alan. 1990. "Artefacts, Memory and a Sense of the Past." In *Collective Remembering*, edited by David Middleton and Derek Edwards. London: Sage Publications.

Rethmann, Petra. 2008. "Nostalgie à Moscou." *Anthropologie et sociétés* 32 (1–2): 85.

Reynolds, Simon. 2012. *Retromania: Pop Culture's Addiction to Its Own Past*. London: Faber & Faber.

Rieff, David. 2018. *Éloge de l'oubli: La mémoire collective et ses pièges*. Clermond-Ferrand: Premier Parallèle.

Robbins, Joel. 2007. "Continuity Thinking and the Problem of Christian Culture: Belief, Time, and the Anthropology of Christianity." *Current Anthropology* 48 (1): 5–38.

Robertson, Roland. 1992. *Globalization: Social Theory and Global Culture*. London: Sage Publications.

Rosaldo, Renato. 1989. "Imperialist Nostalgia." *Representations* 26 (April): 107–122.

Rosen, Lawrence. 1995. *Other Intentions: Cultural Contexts and the Attribution of Inner States*. Santa Fe: School of American Research Press.

Rousso, Henry. 2016. *Face au passé: Essais sur la mémoire contemporaine*. Paris: Belin.

Rubin, Gayle. 1975. "The Traffic in Women: Notes on the 'Political Economy' of Sex." In *Toward an Anthropology of Women*, edited by Reyna Reiter. New York: Monthly Review Press.

Saada, Emmanuelle. 2005. "Entre 'assimilation' et 'décivilisation': L'imitation et le projet colonial républicain." *Terrain* 44: 19–38.

Sahlins, Marshall. 1981. *Historical Metaphors and Mythical Realities: Structure in the Early History of the Sandwich Islands Kingdom*. Ann Arbor: University of Michigan Press.

Salazar, Noel. 2016. "One List, a World of Difference? The Dynamics of Global Heritage at Two Neighbouring Properties." In *World Heritage on the Ground: Ethnographic Perspectives*, edited by Christoph Brumann and David Berliner. Oxford: Berghahn Books.

Sapir, Edward. 1966. *Culture, Language and Personality: Selected Essays*. Berkeley: University of California Press.

———. 1969. *Anthropologie*. Vol. 2. Paris: Les Editions de Minuit.

Sarró, Ramon. 2009. *The Politics of Religious Change on the Upper Guinea Coast: Iconoclasm Done and Undone*. Edinburgh: Edinburgh University Press.

Sartre, Jean-Paul. 1976. *L'être et le néant: Essai d'ontologie phénoménologique*. Paris: Gallimard.

Schäfers, Marlene. 2017. "Writing against Loss: Kurdish Women, Subaltern Authorship, and the Politics of Voice in Contemporary Turkey." *Journal of the Royal Anthropological Institute* 23 (3): 543–561.

Scheper-Hughes, Nancy. 1995. "The Primacy of the Ethical: Propositions for a Militant Anthropology." *Current Anthropology* 36 (3): 409–440.

Schick, Irvin C. 1999. *The Erotic Margin: Sexuality and Spatiality in Alteritist Discourse*. London: Verso.

Scholem, Gershom. 1941. *Major Trends in Jewish Mysticism*. Jerusalem: Schocken Publishing House.

Schönpflug, Ute. 2009. *Cultural Transmission: Psychological, Developmental, Social, and Methodological Aspects*. Cambridge: Cambridge University Press.

Serres, Michel. 2014. *Times of Crisis: What the Financial Crisis Revealed and How to Reinvent Our Lives and Future*. New York: Bloomsbury Academic.

———. 2017. *C'était mieux avant*. Paris: Le Pommier.

Sévéri, Carlo. 2015. *Chimera Principle: An Anthropology of Memory and Imagination*. Chicago: Hau Books.

Shaw, Rosalind. 2002. *Memories of the Slave Trade: Ritual and the Historical Imagination in Sierra Leone*. Chicago: University of Chicago Press.

———. 2007. "Memory Frictions: Localizing the Truth and Reconciliation Commission in Sierra Leone." *International Journal of Transitional Justice* 1 (2): 183–207.

Shepherd, Robert. 2006. "UNESCO and the Politics of Cultural Heritage in Tibet." *Journal of Contemporary Asia* 36 (2): 243–257.

Signoret, Simone. 1978. *La nostalgie n'est plus ce qu'elle était*. Paris: Editions Le Seuil.

Silverman, Helaine. 2011. "Border Wars: The Ongoing Temple Dispute between Thailand and Cambodia and UNESCO's World Heritage List." *International Journal of Heritage Studies* 17 (1): 1–21.

Simmel, Georg. 1898. "Comment les formes sociales se maintiennent." *L'année sociologique*: 71–107.

Spencer, Herbert. 2002. *The Principles of Sociology*. New Brunswick, NJ: Transaction.

Starobinski, J. 1966. "Le concept de nostalgie." *Diogène* 54: 92–115.

Stoczkowski, Wiktor. 2009. "UNESCO's Doctrine of Human Diversity: A Secular Soteriology?" *Anthropology Today* 25 (3): 7–11.

Stoler, Ann Laura. 2002. *Carnal Knowledge and Imperial Power: Race and the Intimate in Colonial Rule*. Berkeley: University of California Press.

Stoller, Paul. 1995. *Embodying Colonial Memories: Spirit Possession, Power, and the Hauka in West Africa*. New York: Routledge.

———. 2009. *The Power of the Between: An Anthropological Odyssey*. Chicago: University of Chicago Press.

Stuart-Fox, Martin. 1997. *A History of Laos*. Cambridge: Cambridge University Press.

Suntikul, Wantanee. 2009. "The Impact of Tourism on the Monks of Luang Prabang." In *Spirit of Place: Between Tangible and Intangible Heritage*, edited by Laurier Turgeon. Québec: Presses de l'Université Laval.

Taussig, Michael. 1984. "Culture of Terror—Space of Death: Roger Casement's Putumayo Report and the Explanation of Torture." *Comparative Studies in Society and History* 26 (3): 467–497.

———. 1993. *Mimesis and Alterity*. London: Routledge.

Tedlock, Barbara. 1991. "From Participant Observation to the Observation of Participation: The Emergence of Narrative Ethnography." *Journal of Anthropological Research* 47 (1): 69–94.

Terdiman, Richard. 1993. *Present Past: Modernity and the Memory Crisis*. Ithaca, NY: Cornell University Press.

Terray, Emmanuel. 2005. *Face aux abus de mémoire*. Arles: Actes Sud.

Theodossopoulos, Dimitrios. 2016a. *Exoticisation Undressed: Ethnographic Nostalgia and Authenticity in Embera Clothes*. Manchester, UK: Manchester University Press.

———. 2016b. "On Ethnographic Nostalgia: Exoticizing and De-exoticizing the Embera, for Example." In *Against Exoticism: Toward the Transcendence of Relativism and Universalism in Anthropology*, edited by Bruce Kapferer and Dimitrios Theodossopoulos. Oxford: Berghahn Books.

Thompson, Michael. 1979. *Rubbish Theory: The Creation and Destruction of Value*. London: Pluto Press.

Todorov, Tzvetan. 1995. *Les abus de la mémoire*. Paris: Arléa.

Tomasello, Michael. 2001. "Cultural Transmission: A View from Chimpanzees and Human Infants." *Journal of Cross-Cultural Psychology* 32 (2): 135–146.

Toren, Christina. 2007. "Sunday Lunch in Fiji: Continuity and Transformation in Ideas of the Household." *American Anthropologist* 109 (2): 285–295.

Touraine, Alain. 2013. *La fin des sociétés*. Paris: Editions Le Seuil.

Tuzin, Donald. 1997. *The Cassowary's Revenge: The Life and Death of Masculinity in a New Guinea Society*. Chicago: University of Chicago Press.

Tylor, Edward. 1994a (1871). *Primitive Culture: Research into the Development of Mythology, Philosophy, Religion, Art and Custom*. Vol. 1. London: Routledge.

———. 1994b (1871). *Primitive Culture: Research into the Development of Mythology, Philosophy, Religion, Art and Custom*. Vol. 2. London: Routledge.

UNESCO. 2004. *Impact: Tourism and Heritage Site Management in the World Heritage Town of Luang Prabang, Lao PDR*. Bangkok: Office of the Regional Advisor for Culture in Asia and the Pacific, UNESCO Bangkok, and School of Travel Industry Management, University of Hawai'i.

Urbain, Jean-Didier. 2003. "Tourisme de mémoire: Un travail de deuil positif." *Les cahiers espaces* 80: 5–7.

Van Alphen, Ernst. 2006. "Second-Generation Testimony, Transmission of Trauma, and Postmemory." *Poetics Today* 27 (2): 473–488.

Wachtel, Nathan. 2011. *Mémoires marranes: Itinéraires dans le sertão du Nordeste brésilien*. La librairie du XXIe siècle. Paris: Editions Le Seuil.

Wacquant, Loïc. 2002. *Corps et âme: Carnets ethnographiques d'un apprenti boxeur*. Marseille: Agone.

———. 2010. "L'habitus comme objet et méthode d'investigation." *Actes de la recherche en sciences sociales* 184 (August): 108–121.

Wang, Shu-Li. 2016. "Civilization and the Transformation of Xiaotun Village at Yin Xu Archaeological Site, China." In *World Heritage on the Ground: Ethnographic Perspectives*, edited by Christoph Brumann and David Berliner. Oxford: Berghahn Books.

Warnier, Jean-Pierre. 2007. *La mondialisation de la culture*. Paris: Editions de La Découverte.

Whitehouse, Harvey. 2004. *Modes of Religiosity: A Cognitive Theory of Religious Transmission*. Walnut Creek, CA: AltaMira Press.

Williams, Patrick. 1993. *Nous, on n'en parle pas: Les vivants et les morts chez les Manouches*. Paris: Editions de la Maison des sciences de l'homme.

Winock, Michel. 2014. *Nationalisme, antisémitisme et fascisme en France*. Paris: Editions Le Seuil.

Winter, Tim. 2007. *Post-Conflict Heritage, Postcolonial Tourism: Culture, Politics and Development at Angkor*. London: Routledge.

Zempléni, Andras. 1976. "La chaîne du secret." *Nouvelle revue de psychanalyse* 14: 313–324.

Index

acceleration, 7, 107n2

accelerism, 3

acquiring new knowledge: and ethnography, 17–18; imitation, 87–88

Allison, Anne, 85, 105

anxiety: about irreversibility, 101; of losing cultural diversity, 4; and the self, 94

apocalypse, 7–8

apocalyptic beliefs, 15

Appadurai, Arjun, 4, 77, 107n9, 119n53

architects, 41–43, 51–52

architecture, 52; and reproduction, 100

Aristotle, 16, 87

Auschwitz-Birkenau, 37

authenticity, 4, 38–39, 40; and modernity, 32; and objects, 19; and value of a site, 41–43

Baga, 20–22; in the Guinean coast, 112n1; in a non-Bulongic environment, 30; traditional culture of, 33–34

Balandier, Georges, 74

Bangkok: British expats in, 48; bureaucratic nostalgia, 62; and UNESCO, 41–42

Barth, Fredrik, 13

Bartholeyns, Gils, 105, 107n11

Bastide, Roger, 73, 118n36

Baudelaire, Charles, 4, 36, 107n10

Benjamin, Walter, 6, 100

Bhabha, Homi, 17, 112n78

Bloch, Maurice, 111n68

Bokaré, Asékou, 21, 24

Bortolotto, Chiara, 38, 105

Bourdieu, Pierre, 13–14, 112n70

Bourgois, Philippe, 85–86, 88, 90, 120n29, 120n37; and crack dealers, 93; *In Search of Respect*, 80

Boyer, Dominic, 115n16

Boym, Svetlana, 117n11

Brumann, Christoph, 38, 105, 110n49, 114nn5–6, 121n4

Buddhas of Bamiyan, 101

Buddhism in Luang Prabang, 1–2, 39–41, 48–50; celebrations, 59–60; in the future, 63. *See also* Tak Baad

Bulongic: dance, 32–33; early ethnography, 67; globalization of, 34–35; history, 23–25; identity, 26–30; masks, 21; people of New Guinea, 11, 15; ritual practices, 21–23; women, 31–32. *See also* Baga: in the Guinean coast; Paulme, Denise

bureaucracy, 36–65; and UNESCO rhetoric, 42–43

Butler, Judith, 102, 122n21

Carsten, Janet, 76, 118n52

Cassin, Barbara, 3, 107n4

catastrophes, 77; catastrophism, 7; catastrophist perspective, 66–67

chameleon, the human, 18, 81, 86–89, 93–95

Chichen Itza, 37

143

loss (cont.)
of the environment, 109n40;
experience and trauma of, 7, 109n33;
fear of, 72; forgetting, 23; irreversibility, 42; of knowledge, 28; of an
object, 20; personal, 72, 101; of
power, 11, 27, 29–30; and transmission, 10–16, 109n33; remedies against,
15; resistance to, 45–46, 50; Tak Baad,
as a symbol, 60
Luang Prabang, 1, 11, 36, 40; loss,
in, 51–54; Miss Luang Prabang,
55–56; nostalgia, 61–65; territorial
dispute, 122n19; tourism, 48–50.
See also experts: in Luang Prabang; gay
tourism in Luang Prabang; heterotopia; *kathoey*; Laos: women; nostalgia;
UNESCO: UNESCOization

Malinowski, Bronislaw, 66–67, 69,
71–72, 80, 89; *Diary*, 80;
Malinowskian era, 85
manhood, 21
Marcus, George, 68
mask, 19, 20–24, 31–32; for circumcision, 27; for initiation, 34; and spirits,
28. *See also* Mossolo Kombo
Mauss, Marcel, 69; "Techniques of the
Body," 12
Mbembe, Achille, *Critique de la raison
nègre*, 19
Mekong, 43, 49, 57
melancholy, 3, 68, 94
Memmi, Albert, 17
memory, 2, 7, 9, 11, 19–20, 24, 99; of
African slaves, 73, 75; of elders,
25–26; policies, 98; sciences of,
109n44; societal, 76–77; of tensions,
102; transmission and heritage, 100;
vicarious, 109–110n48; within
objects, 20, 112–113n2
Meskell, Lynnn, 38, 105
mimesis, 16–17; mimetic abilities, 17–18;
mimetic process, 16

modernity, 7, 23, 32, 35, 49, 52–53, 56, 61,
67, 75–77, 79; modernization, 9, 43,
49, 74, 78
Mossolo Kombo, 24–29; in Conakry
life, 34; globalization, 34; initiation,
27, 29, 31; mask, 21; mask dance, 24;
nostalgia, 27; secrets, 22–25
museum, 19–20, 23, 35, 72; eco-museum,
4; in Laos, 47; museum studies, 2
museumification, 9, 51

nationalism, 10, 56, 103; and populism,
108n18
Naumescu, Vlad, 15, 105
neoliberalism, 80
nostalgia, 1, 3–5, 7–9, 17, 35, 72, 74, 100;
anthropological, 78–80; bureaucratic,
36–65; business, 50; consumerist,
64–65, 107n3; ethnographic, 23;
experts, 42–43, 50, 62–63; for Laos,
46, 58; for Luang Prabang, 39, 42–43,
48–50, 54, 62–63; for Mossolo
Kombo, 27, 29; militant, 43–46, 62;
patrimonial, 64, 96; for the primitive,
9; UNESCO and globalization, 53;
vicarious, 68–69. *See also* exonostalgia; endonostalgia; heritage;
memory; tourism
nostalgiascape, 63

Ogien, Ruwen, 92–93, 105
Onfray, Michel, 108n18

Papua, 6, 66, 83, 113n9
participant observation, 17, 79, 81, 92,
120n27
participation, 83–87, 90, 94–95, 103
passéisme, 63
past, the, 2–4, 7–9, 12–15, 20, 22–27, 30,
32–35, 39, 50, 68–71, 73–76, 100,
109n48; colonial, 42, 64, 75;
experienced, 62–63; idealized, 3, 49,
53; Indochinese, 64; objects,
112–113n2; pre-Islamic, 30, 102;

About the Author

DAVID BERLINER is a Belgian anthropologist. He is a professor at the Université Libre de Bruxelles. From 2001 to 2003, he completed a postdoctoral fellowship at Harvard University, and has taught at the Central European University in Hungary. Between 2011 and 2015, he was coeditor of *Social Anthropology/Anthropologie Sociale*, the journal of the European Association of Social Anthropologists. His books include *Mémoires religieuses Baga* and the edited volumes *World Heritage on the Ground* (with Christoph Brumann), *Anthropology and Nostalgia* (with Olivia Angé), and *Learning Religion* (with Ramon Sarró).